"Elvis"

Special Memories

Of Living and Working With
The Man We Called
"Our Friend"

By
Donnie Sumner and Ed Hill

A host of books have been written about
"The King Of Rock And Roll"
but seldom has **ELVIS** been portrayed as the
"Fun Loving and Loyal Friend"
that he truly was and
"that"is the purpose of this collection of
"Our Personal Memories."

During the years we worked and lived with
ELVIS,
we made an immeasurable number of memories with
the man we knew as
"OUR FRIEND"

Some of them,
we gladly share with anyone who wishes to listen.
Some of them,
we hold sacred and will only talk about them when we
"Meet ELVIS Once Again"
and we get to reminisce and laugh
"TOGETHER"

donniesumner @ bellsouth.net   edhill4u @ yahoo.com

"ELVIS"
Special Memories

By
Donnie Sumner *and* Ed Hill

ISBN-13: 978-1532737138 - ISBN-10: 1532737130

All Rights Reserved

Printed In U.S.A.

Table Of Contents

Donnie Sumner

*W*ith a career spanning more than fifty years, Donnie continues to carry on the *"Southern Gospel"* tradition.

Donnie is the nephew of the late *J. D. SUMNER*, who was nationally acclaimed as the "*world's lowest bass singer.*" Both Donnie and J. D. were very *"close friends"* with *ELVIS PRESLEY* and sang on both his stage appearances and his recordings. Donnie was the lead vocalist with both *"J.D. Sumner and the Stamps Quartet"* and his own group, *"Voice Inc."*

Sumner is noted as one of America's most renowned inspirational composers and in 1970, he received the *G.M.A.'s* prestigious *DOVE AWARD* for *"Gospel Song of the Year,"* In 1969 Donnie was awarded the *S.E.S.A.C. AWARD* as *"Best Country Songwriter."* In 1970 he was nominated for a *GRAMMY AWARD* by *N.A.R.A.S.* for *"Country Song of the Year."* Donnie was also afforded the honor of having a solo appearance in the Elvis documentary, *"ELVIS ON TOUR"* in which he was featured on the gospel song, *"THE LIGHTHOUSE"*.

Late in 1972, Donnie resigned from the Stamps Quartet, organized his own group, *VOICE INC.* and was asked by Elvis to again become a part of his entourage and to join his *personal "family."* Donnie became a constant house guest, a close companion, and a stage associate to his *"friend" Elvis*. Donnie was responsible for all of Elvis' background vocal arrangements and on a nightly basis would perform *"gospel tunes"* to Elvis in private *"living room"* sessions at Elvis' request.

Often, Elvis would ask Donnie to sing one of his *"own"* original love songs. It was from such occasions that Elvis eventually came to record two of Donnie's country songs. *"MR. SONG MAN"* and *"I MISS YOU."*

For over thirty years, Donnie's efforts have been devoted to sharing the *"good news"* that God loves them and desires greatly to be their closest and most reliable companion.

Ed Hill

*F*or nearly sixty years, Ed Hill has enjoyed a distinguished career as a *"Southern Gospel baritone singer."* In 1959 Ed organized a group known as the *"Prophets Quartet"* and remained with them as their manager and baritone singer until late 1973.

Early in 1974, *"J.D. Sumner," "The World's Lowest Bass Singer,"* asked Ed to come join him as the baritone singer for *"J.D. Sumner and the Stamps Quartet."* He continued as their baritone vocalist until The Stamps disbanded following the death of their leader, J.D. Sumner, in 1998.

The Stamps Quartet was part of the *Elvis* entourage when Ed joined the group and because of his quiet manner and gentlemanly ways, Elvis took an immediate liking to him and Ed became one of *"Elvis' very close and dear friends."*

In addition to his musical abilities, Ed is well remembered and loved by the Elvis fans for another contribution he made to the Elvis show. Ask any *"Elvis fan"* if they are familiar with the following quotation, *"Ladies and gentlemen, Elvis has left the building. Thank you and good night!"* and, without exception, they will recognize it as the *"ending announcement"* at all *"Elvis Presley concerts."* Ed Hill is the gentleman who made the announcement at the close of each Elvis performance.

As a member of The Stamps Quartet, the group that toured with, recorded with and backed up Elvis for the last seven years of his life, Ed is well aware of Elvis' *"human side"* as-well-as Elvis' genuine *"love of Gospel music."* It has been well documented that Elvis loved gospel music and he allowed the Stamps Quartet to open each Elvis show with thirty minutes of their *"own Gospel songs."*

Ed is still pursuing his love for Gospel Quartet music and travels nationwide as the baritone voice in a well-known quartet known as *"The Songfellows."*

Dedication

*H*i! I'm ***Donnie Sumner*** and I'm ***Ed Hill*** and we were both blessed enough to be afforded the joyful privilege of being able to call:

"Elvis" our "friend."

During the years that we lived, travelled and sang with Elvis, we accumulated a vast collection of wonderful memories and it has been our pleasure recalling a few

of them, *"especially for you!"*

Neither of us would have en-joyed our life with Elvis had it not been for our *"hero"* and *"boss:"*

"The World's Lowest Bass Singer"
"J.D. Sumner."

J.D. was gracious enough
"to give us both a position in The Stamps Quartet."

He was loving enough
"to take us under his wing."

He was patient enough
"to teach us the art of stage presentation."

He was considerate enough
"to overlook our mistakes."

*F*or all the memories, the friendships and the multitude of other blessings that have come our way because he crossed the paths of our lives; *We dedicate this entire collection of memories as a tribute to the memory of:*

"Our Beloved Friend"
"J.D. Sumner"

"When I was a child, ladies and gentleman, I was a dreamer.
I read comic books, and I was a hero in the movie;
So every dream that I ever dreamed
has come true a hundred times."

"I learned very early in life
that without a song,
the day would never end;
without a song,
a man ain't got a friend;
without a song,
the road would never bend;
without a song.
So I keep singing a song."

"Goodnight ... Thank You."

Elvis Presley
January 16, 1971

The Measure Of A Man

TO YOU ALL ... *"OUR FAITHFUL ELVIS FRIENDS:"*

Without *"YOU"* the fans, there could be no *"US"* the performers. You have honored us by allowing us the privilege to call you *"OUR FRIENDS."*

"THANK YOU" for the memories you have made possible

Often times, I have pondered upon what is meant by the phrase, *"A Real Man."*

Resting quietly in my memories, I can find the true attributes of a real man as they were portrayed in the man we all loved and knew as: *"ELVIS PRESLEY. "*

To most philanthropists, *"GIVING KINDNESS"* is done for social, economic or political reasons. A *"REAL GIVER"* gives expecting nothing in return other than a warm feeling for having done good for *"goodness sake."*

"FRIENDSHIP" is often used in an attempt to receive something that one needs at a particular moment. A *"TRUE FRIEND"* will hang with you in the dark times, cry with you in the sad times, laugh with you in the happy times and unconditionally love you regardless of the situation. All the time, expecting only the reward of knowing that they were there for you.

In today's world of situational ethics, *"CHARACTER"* has been reduced to varying shades of grey. Never-the-less, a man of *"REAL CHARACTER"* honors the merit of his word as his vow. It's *"REAL CHARACTER"* that motivates a man to strive toward making the corner of his daily world a better place for others. It's *"REAL CHARACTER"* that causes a *"Super-Star"* to make a Mayor wait in his dressing room until he concludes a conversation with an auditorium janitor. It's *"REAL CHARACTER"* that causes a man of means to give a brand new Cadillac to an unknown mother and then just smile and walk away. It's *"REAL CHARACTER"* that forces a man to stand to his feet and single-handedly confront a danger approaching a close friend.

Among all the attributes attributed to the making of a *"REAL MAN,"* I have concluded that there are three head the list:

> *"True Kindness"*
> *"Unconditional Friendship"*
> and
> *"Personal Character"*

I once lived with a
"REAL MAN"
and his name was

**"ELVIS
PRESLEY."**

- Donnie Sumner

Elvis

was born to sing;

His life was a song

but He died in silence.

If the melody is to continue:

WE MUST BE THE MUSIC.

Off To A Beautiful Start

Some folks know how to make an *"entrance."* Others have the ability to make a *"grand entrance."* Then there's the *"super grand entrance."*

Very few personalities have been able to master the latter but *"Elvis did!"*

It was about 7:00 P.M. on November 2, 1971, in Minneapolis, Minnesota at the Hilton Hotel. Elvis was scheduled to start a tour on November 5 and The Stamps, along with all the other members of the Elvis stage troupe, had been in the hotel ballroom since about *"two o'clock"* that afternoon waiting to begin the first of two six hour rehearsals. Needless to say, everyone in the room was excited as we anxiously awaited Elvis' arrival. This was to be my first tour with Elvis and I'm tellin' ya the truth, *"I couldn't hardly wait to get started!"*

All of us in the room were quite startled when the ballroom doors burst open like a car had hit them and *"Joe Esposito,"* Elvis' personal confidante, came thru the door hollering:

"Ladies and gentlemen, Elvis is 'IN' the building!"

In line behind Joe, playfully pushing him out of the way, were Elvis' two chief bodyguards, *"Red West"* and *"Sonny West:"* And then:

There He Was!
"ELVIS!"

Standing in the doorway dressed in an *"Elvis-design"* light blue suit, wearing a white shirt with his signatory *"high collar"* and frilly cuffs, sporting a light blue velvet, *"Beal Street,"* hat and carrying a black cane with a big golden carved ornament on the top of it, *"Elvis was something to behold!"* It was then I heard Elvis yell out, *"What time does this 'two o'clock' session start?"*

After taking his hat off and throwing it over to Sonny, he handed his cane to Red and then proceeded to shake the hand of each musician in the room. I wish I could express the feeling I

had when Elvis stepped in front of me, reached out his hand to shake mine and said, *"Hi Donnie, glad to have ya in the family!"*

"Family!"

That's what it really came to be.

For the next six years I would come to know Elvis in ways that very few fellows ever had the privilege to experience.

Millions knew the name and experienced the persona of a superstar the world called, *"Elvis Presley"* but I have the joy-filled memory of having known Elvis as *"my friend."*

In my lifetime I have worked for numerous employers and I can truthfully say that I never developed a more deeply rooted *"friendship"* or ever had a greater *"respect"* for one's abilities than the brotherly bond and high regard which was to be created by my relationship with Elvis. *"He was a 'great boss' and a 'true friend'."*

During my years with Elvis, I would see more big cities, fly in more planes, stand before more people, shake more hands and receive more applause than I could ever have dreamed of.

The entire world knew Elvis as the *"King of Rock"* but I truly wish they all could have known the Elvis I call, *"my friend!"*

I have memories galore. Some of them I will share with anyone who wishes to listen. Some of them, I will hold sacred and only recall when Elvis and I, *"once again:"*

Meet and Reminisce Together.

- Donnie Sumner

A Warm Memory
Can Turn Raindrops Into Sunbeams

"Don't Lose Your Marbles"

"He's lost his marbles!"

At times I've heard that said about me following something crazy I had just done or said and there was one occasion when I thought the same thing about myself!

It happened at the close of my first rehearsal with Elvis on November 2, 1971, in Minneapolis, Minnesota. In my opinion, that first rehearsal was a disaster. In the words of my friend, *"Joe Guercio,"* Elvis' orchestra conductor, *"It was like watching a Russian movie with Chinese dialogue."*

Elvis really liked the harmony and the extremely wide vocal range of *"The Stamps Quartet"* and because I had done all of the Stamps

arranging, he asked *"me"* to be in charge of telling all the background vocalists what their particular parts were gonna be.

The Elvis background ensemble consisted of three ladies, *"The Sweet Inspirations,"* four guys, *"The Stamps Quartet"* plus *"J.D. Sumner"* and *"Kathy Westmoreland."* Parts of the responsibility were easy, especially the *"hand-clappin'."*

On the older Elvis' songs we simply had to *"Bop-Doo-Wah-Duh"* or *"Ooh and Ah"* in what is referred to as *"block harmony."* Of course, between these rhythmic words, there was a lot of *"clappin'!"* On these songs it was pretty much just, *"find a note and have fun."*

No problem, so far!

For this new tour, several big production numbers had been added to Elvis' previous Las Vegas *"song line-up"* in order to better accent his great vocal skills. Songs such as, *"My Way,"* *"You Gave Me A Mountain,"* *"American Trilogy"* and *"How Great Thou Art,"* among others. These type tunes required more precision than the *"hang on and have a ball"* songs that had made Elvis a national, *"rock-a-billy"* icon.

Along with the *"big songs"* came *"big problems!"*

Elvis really liked the extremely high, lyrical obligatos of Kathy Westmoreland. He also enjoyed the carefree style and rhythmic interpretations of The Sweet Inspirations.

Elvis had chosen J.D. Sumner and The Stamps for our close harmony and also, because *"J.D., had been his childhood hero."*

In addition to the nine of us *"Charlie Hodge"* was on board singing all the duets with Elvis.

Each of our styles were totally different and we couldn't quite *"git it together!"* It was sort'a like trying to push a rope!

To further aggravate the problem, The Stamps had *"two bass"* singers. Earlier that year, J.D. had hired *"Richard Sterban"* as the bass singer for The Stamps and *"J.D."* had become our *"featured soloist."* When we joined Elvis, J.D. had only planned to travel along with the Stamps as our own *"Colonel Parker."*

As soon as our first rehearsal started, Elvis quickly and very definitely made it known that he wanted J.D. in the group so he could do, what he referred to as, *"those B-59 bomber,"* zoom endings that was J.D.'s signatory vocal move. As always, when Elvis made a request, it became a swift reality and J.D. was suddenly part of the background vocals.

I was the lead vocalist for The Stamps and generally sang the melody of our songs. In this case, Elvis was singing *"all"* of the melody lines and every time I opened my mouth to sing, I was on *"Elvis' part."*

After about an hour of rehearsing, I finally came up with a plan.

For the majority of all ballads, I asked *"Kathy Westmoreland"* to sing all of the melodies an octave above *"Myrna Smith"* of The Sweet Inspirations because Kathy could absolutely sing thru the roof and I asked *"J.D."* to sing an octave below *"Richard Sterban,"* The Stamps bass vocalist, *"which for J.D. was no problem at all."*

For the most part, when singing harmonies together, The Sweet Inspirations were to sing louder than The Stamps on all of the fast songs and vice-versa on all of the slower ballads and the gospel type tunes. At that point, it pretty much began to level out and in a short time we had developed a rather nice sounding group.

As for me, my voice was *"jumpin' and dodgin' all night"* trying to avoid Elvis' lead vocal line but somehow, we managed to get to the end of the rehearsal without anyone noticing my inability to fit in.

At the close of the rehearsal Elvis went around giving each of us a moment of personal attention. During the time he was talking to me he asked, *"How ya think it went, Donnie?"*

I responded by assuring him that it was coming together and everyone was *"gittin' the hang of it."* I concluded my response with, *"That is, everybody 'cept me! Tryin' to find a part that won't get in your way is like tryin' to find a marble in a bucket a' pearls!"*

Elvis laughed that cute little laugh of his and replied, *"Don't worry 'bout it! Just sing what ever ya want and when I point to ya, sing somethin' high."*

The next night, just before we started our second rehearsal, Elvis' stepbrother, *"Ricky Stanley,"* came over to me and said, *"The boss told me to give this to ya"* and he handed me a nice little wooden box with a small golden clasp holding it shut.

I opened the clasp, lifted the lid and looked inside. The box contained a handful of marbles. On top of the collection there was a note in Elvis' handwriting. The note read, *"You're here to stay, don't lose your marbles!"*

When the tour was over I gave the marbles to my son, Jeff. Since then, I assume that Jeff either traded them for steelies or my daughter, Robin, secured them in the bottom of her fish bowl. At this point, I have no idea where they are hiding but with their disappearance, I can state for the record:

At least once in my life:
"I really did lose my marbles!"

- Donnie Sumner

Success is:
"Climbing out of a hole,
Without Getting Dirty!"

Welcome To The Family

"*Donnie, if you had a ring on ya thumbs, you'd have 'em all covered!*"

That's what my father-in-law said to me at a family meal during Christmas of 1975.

I had been working with Elvis since 1973 and because of Elvis' generous gifts, I had acquired a considerable collection of beautiful jewelry.

On numerous occasions, especially on the closing night of each Elvis tour: Elvis would have his Memphis, Tennessee jeweler, *"Lowell Hayes,"* come visit us. Lowell would invariably bring with him several cases of exquisite jewelry. Elvis would take all the cases of jewelry and personally unpack each of them, piece by piece. He enjoyed carefully arranging each piece according to its style and setting. Once everything had been unpacked, Elvis would either display them on a covered table or place his arrangements on a carpeted floor.

I can't express how it felt to hear Elvis say to everyone in the room, **"O.K. Boys and girls, pick out what 'cha want!"** You should have been there! Each of us acted like, *"a monkey with a new wrist watch."* All of us, *"everyone at the same time,"* would reach out to pick up a piece, try it on, look at it and then choose another item and then go through the same process.

When everybody was sufficiently pleased with their choices, Elvis would have Lowell *"tally up"* the cost of everything that had been removed from the collection and then he would have *"Joe Espisito,"* his personal assistant, write Lowell a check for that amount.

By Christmas of 1975, I had been on a lot of tours with Elvis and had amassed a large collection of *"tour rings."* Wearing eight of them at a time was just too overwhelming for my, above mentioned, *"ultra conservative"* Father-in-law.

Each piece of tour jewelry that Elvis gave to me was accepted as a gracious and wonderful gift. It was even more humbling when He would call you aside somewhere and present you with a gift that he had personally chosen just for you. As we say in the south, ***"That'll knock ya hat in the creek!"***

 In 1974, Elvis designed and gave each member of J.D. Sumner and the Stamps Quartet a pair of ***"sunglasses,"*** mounted in a 14K brushed gold frame with ***"our individual names,"*** in silver letters, on the right earpiece and the word, ***"Stamps"*** of matching design, on the left earpiece. Can you imagine the feeling that ***"you"*** would have, walking thru a crowd with Elvis: With you wearing a pair of sunglasses *"exactly like his"* with the exception of the name embossed on the side. ***"I always felt that same way!"***

In 1975, Elvis gifted each of us in the Stamps Quartet with a custom designed, 14K ***"gold nugget ring"*** with the name ***"Stamps"*** inlaid in silver across the top. Without a doubt ***"The Stamps Ring"*** was the largest ring on either of my hands.

The only finger I had that was big enough to handle it was the middle finger on my right hand. Sometimes, I think that the weight of my ***"Stamps Ring"*** might be why my right arm is one eighth of an inch longer than my left.

 Of all the jewelry that Elvis gave to me, one piece holds top place in my memories.

Right after The Stamps joined Elvis, in 1973, we were singing for him in his Graceland living room and ***"Charlie Hodge"*** came into the piano room and he was carrying five black velvet boxes. Charlie handed all five of them to Elvis who then presented a box to each member of the Stamps. I can't express, nor will I ever forget, the feeling that flooded over me when Elvis came to stand in front me, then open up my little black box, take out the gift of a ***"beautiful 14K gold necklace"*** and hang my *"T.C.B."* around my neck. It made the moment even more memorable when he said to me, ***"Welcome to the family, Donnie!"***

And *"Family"* is what *"We Really Were!"*

- Donnie Sumner

The Love Behind A Gift

IS BETTER THAN THE GIFT ITSELF

What Was Elvis Like

*I*t's difficult to teach an old man the skills needed for the *"Social Media"* world. Never-the-less, I finally learned how to navigate my way through the maze of *"emails, friends, likes and blogs!"*

A while back, I sent out a questionnaire to all of my friends around the world and asked them to submit a one line question they would like for me to address in this compilation of personal memoirs regarding my life with *"Elvis."* I was surprised by the number of emails I received in return.

I was further surprised when four questions covered more than ninety percent of the responses. One of these was, *"What was Elvis like?"* I frequently respond to this question in a comical manner by saying, *"He was the best looking, most talented and richest 'cotton picker' I ever met!"*

In truth, Elvis was a multi-faceted individual and each element in his world was quite unique.

"Elvis, the *SUPERSTAR*" was an entertainer's role model!

He was a man who had risen to the zenith of the entertainment business from a life of poverty. Unlike most stars I have known, in the process of *"becoming famous"* he never forgot those who were with him at the beginning. His childhood buddies were some of his closest associates. To those of us who knew him best, he was not only a star, he was our friend and a buddy. He knew what he wanted on stage and we tried to give it to him. He was not demanding but we reacted to his wishes freely. We respected his position as a *"superstar"* and he most graciously recognized our supportive roles.

Because of my friendship with Elvis I have had the privilege of being in the company of numerous big stars and in my opinion no one ever played the *"star role"* with greater poise and grace than Elvis did. Whether it was on stage, in his home, hanging around with guys or being a boss, Elvis was always kind, considerate and gracious to all of us. To each of us, he was definitely *"number one"* but it was *"not"* by his *"demand."* Respect was our personal choice and it was freely given. We all admired him for *"what"* he was and not because of *"who"* he was.

"Elvis, the *SINGER*" was a great vocalist?

I have both studied and taught voice. I have also had the opportunity to teach vocal pedagogy which is simply teaching teachers and I can assure you that Elvis was a great singer. His singing voice was not all that mature when he began his career but thru the years, Elvis perfected all of the qualities necessary to achieve the status of both **"great vocalist"** and **"excellent performer."**

The average singing range is about one and a half octaves. Elvis had a singing range of nearly three octaves. The breath control of a singer determines the volume of their tones and the length with which they can sustain them. When it was needed, Elvis' voice could be extra ordinarily loud and he could hold a note longer than anyone I have ever known.

All singers strive for clarity of diction and perfection of communication. Very few artists acquire both with excellence but **"Elvis did."** You could understand every word he sang and when he was finished, you understood the entire message of the song. In the music industry we call this **"milking a song"** and Elvis had this ability in great quantity.

No one gets excited when a singer is motionless and the art of **"stage presence"** is something rather unheard of in today's music industry. Most everything is choreographed and done in unison with others. There is very little action which is uniquely personal. Elvis **"commanded the stage"** when he performed. Everything he did was unique to him alone. Whether it was an eye movement, arm thrust or leg motion it was **"All Elvis!"** Elvis was definitely a skilled vocalist and a superlative performer.

"Elvis, the *ATHELETE*" was a very skilled, competitive and formidable opponent to be reckoned with.

Some folks choose to believe that Elvis' karate skills were not truly authentic. I can assure you that they were. I have seen him do unbelievable katas in the art form and if you had been present, then you, like myself, would have become a true admirer of his martial arts ability.

I have seen Elvis spar with some of the biggest names in the martial arts arena and without exception, **"Elvis was able to 'best' them all!"** I recall one night in Las Vegas, when during one of Elvis' dinner shows at the Hilton Hotel, he proved his abilities beyond any doubt.

Karate schools are referred to as Dojo's and one of Elvis' close associates, *"Ken Parker,"* owned such a facility in Los Angeles. True *"masters"* of the karate form are addressed as *"Sifu"* when approached by another practioner of the art. Both Elvis and Ken Parker were respectfully addressed as *"Sifu."*

There was a rival dojo in Los Angeles, whose students had lost numerous competitions to some of the students from the dojo that Ken Parker owned.

On this particular night, in the Vegas Hilton showroom, four of the leading instructors from the rival dojo were in attendance. They knew that Elvis was a large sponsor of the Ken Parker dojo and they wanted to show Elvis that their style of karate was more efficient than the Kenpo style that he and Ed practiced. Consequently, during Elvis' show they

suddenly jumped on the stage and all four of them simultaneously came at Elvis from four different points. The bodyguards, *"Red West, Sonny West, Dick Grobe and Dave Hebler,"* came rushing to Elvis' defense.

The bodyguards were surprised when Elvis ordered them to *"stand down."* Then Elvis, *"single-handedly,"* came to his own defense. The sight was something to behold. Elvis kicked one of his attackers in the chest so hard that it caused his arms to fly up with so much force, his watch was torn from his wrist, went sailing off toward my side of the stage and came to rest directly beneath my stool. I might add, *"I still have the watch!"* Suffice it to say, *"All four gentlemen were removed from the building by emergency vehicles and spend a measure of time in both the hospital E.R. section and later, within the luxury of the Las Vegas penal facility."*

Elvis also loved raquetball and became very skilled in the sport. I never volunteered to play a game with him because they told me that Elvis used to enjoy kidding his opponent by hitting his back side with the raquetball. They also assured me that Elvis was extremely accurate with his aim. I assumed that the hit would sting considerably and I have a delicate bottom, so I refrained from offering my physical prowess.

"Elvis, the *MAN*" was the side of Elvis that we all loved the most.

Once the lights went out, the fans were gone and the jump suit was in the closet, my favorite Elvis came into view. Wearing relaxed clothes, sporting an imperfect hair do, simply laying back on the coach with his feet on the coffee table and laughing: *"That's the Elvis I most often recall."*

When all of the accolades have been voiced and when all the compliments have been noted, the bottom line becomes a simple statement.

Elvis was,
above all other things:
"A Kind and Considerate Friend!"

- Donnie Sumner

It takes more than whiskers
to make a man;
Nothing does the trick like:

"A Loving Heart"
and
"A Helping Hand"

Elvis' Love For Gospel Music

"A tree never falls far from its roots."

Elvis' first exposure to the joy of music came to him as a very young child in Tupelo, Mississippi. Early in life he became enamored with both the message and the spirit of *"Gospel"* music as he would sit outside a small church, not far from his humble home, and listen to its black congregation fill the evening with their exuberant singing of *"Gospel"* songs.

Later in life, Elvis came into contact with the *"blues"* genre and eventually combined the two styles into one and now the world enjoys, what has become known worldwide as the *"Elvis style"* of musical delivery.

Although his fame was created by what has been classed as *"rock-a-billy,"* Elvis never lost or forsook his initial love for the sound of a *"good 'ol Gospel song."*

I find it fascinating, that with all the recordings released by Elvis during his lifetime, he was only recognized three times by the National Association of Recording Arts and Science *(NARAS)* in the form of *"Grammy Awards."* Each of them was for a *"Gospel"* album: *"Best Sacred Performance,"* 1967; *"Best Inspirational Performance,"* 1972 and *"Best Inspirational Song,"* 1974.

On numerous occasions, friends ask me why Elvis loved *"Gospel"* music so much. The answer comes very quickly, *"It's the words."* Gospel music is the only genre of musical composition containing lyrical content that *"truly encourages, soothes and gives the listener hope for a brighter tomorrow."*

For nearly six years I had the pleasure of singing this form of music to Elvis on a nightly basis and in that context, I have witnessed, *"first hand,"* the calming attributes of *"Gospel"* lyrics.

I joined Elvis in 1971 and at that time he seemed to always be *"happy-go-lucky"* and at peace with the world. Shortly after my joining the group, he seemed to be going thru an emotional change. In 1973, his marriage was officially dissolved and he became less and less carefree. During the daylight hours, Elvis was always laughing and joking but when night time settled in on us he would become quieter and quieter as the evening progressed.

No one in our *"family group"* was more keenly aware of Elvis' emotional swings than his closest friend, "*Charlie Hodge."* Amid all of the frivolity of Elvis' *"den,"* at some point, every night without exception, Charlie could detect that Elvis' thoughts were somewhere other than with us and he would quietly slip over to the piano and start playing a soft

"Gospel" song of his choice. Charlie's piano playing was an unspoken invitation for my group, Voice, to come over and join him around the piano and sing along. When we would start to sing, Elvis would invariably come over and join us. He enjoyed singing the *"bass"* part for our *"living room quartet."* Elvis generally didn't sing too long and he would soon slip into his *"listening"* chair, sit down and start calling out the titles of the songs he wanted Voice to sing for him. He always listened intently to the words of each song and would often ask us to repeat a particular line or a complete portion of a given set of lyrics. As the songs continued to be sung, it was very apparent that Elvis was enjoying the music and anyone present could readily observe that his spirit was being elevated. We never sang to Elvis less than an hour and frequently continued on until the wee hours of the morning. Charlie could always tell when Elvis was *"O.K."* again and in order to close out the evening, without Elvis having to do so, he would stand up, stretch real big and in a humorous manner say something like, *"Let's take up an offering and be dismissed!"* Elvis would always laugh real big at whatever Charlie did at that point and would stand up and say something like, *"Sounds good to me! I'm gonna call it a day!"* Then off to bed he would go for a *"peaceful"* nights sleep.

A lot of different answers have been offered in regard to the question, *"What was Elvis' 'favorite' Gospel song?"* Well, boys and girls, I can

tell you, *"as a fact,"* because *"I sang them to him every night for a long time."*

There were, roughly, about thirty to forty tunes that I recall Elvis listening to during my years of singing to him at night. Some were sung infrequently, others were sung very often and then there were several that we sang *"every night, without exception."* Among the list of all the songs that Voice sang to Elvis, *"two"* stand out above all the rest. Not a night went by without multiplied renditions of the two songs: *"Come Ye Disconsolate"* and *"In The Sweet Bye And Bye."* I remember one night when Voice sang *"In The Sweet Bye And Bye"* eighteen times back to back.

 If, for just a moment, you can imagine Elvis as just an *"ordinary man,"* experiencing *"ordinary sadness"* by reason of a broken family relationship and then read the *"lyrics"* that brought to him such *"extra ordinary comfort;"* Hopefully, you will understand why I consider the *"two"* songs that Elvis

"most often wanted to hear,"

to be:

"Elvis' Favorite Gospel Songs!"

"Come Ye Disconsolate"* and *"In The Sweet Bye And Bye"

COME YE DISCONSOLATE

Come ye disconsolate where-e'er ye lanquish
Come to the mercy-seat fervently kneel
Here bring your wounded hearts
Here tell your anquish
Earth has no sorrow that Heaven cannot heal

Joy of the desolate light of the straying
Hope of the penitent fadeless and pure
Here speaks the Comforter
Tenderly saying
Earth has no sorrow that Heaven cannot cure

Here see the Bread of Life see waters flowing
Forth from the throne of God pure from above
Come to the feast of love
Come ever knowing
Earth has no sorrow that Heaven can't remove

IN THE SWEET BYE AND BYE

There's a land that is fairer than day
And by faith we can see it afar
And the Father waits over the way
He's prepared us a dwelling place there

We shall sing on that beautiful shore
The melodious song of the blest
And our spirits shall sorrow no more
Not a sigh for the blessings of rest

In the sweet bye and bye
We shall meet on that beautiful shore
In the sweet bye and bye
We shall meet on that beautiful shore

I have sung these two songs over and over again for Elvis as he would quietly sit in his *"listening"* chair and savor the *"lyrics."* I know it's an impossibility, but if I could, at this point in time:

I would sing them to Elvis again:
"All night," if he wanted me to!

- Donnie Sumner

You Can Always
PLEASE YOURSELF
by
PLEASING SOMEONE ELSE

It's All In The Name

"Hi! My name's Donnie!" and the world says, *"Donnie who?"*

"Hi! I'm Elvis!" and the people start screaming!

The difference between the two responses is readily apparent, *"It's all in the name"*

The closest I ever came to the latter response is with the line, *"Hello, I'm Donnie Sumner and I welcome you to the 'Elvis Presley Show'!"* Over

eight hundred times I had the joyful privilege of using that phrase as my group *"Voice Inc."* and I sang the opening set on all of Elvis' shows. I was always amazed at the reception I received when lean, lanky, long-haired and sometimes misbehaved *"lil' ol' me"* was afforded the privilege of associating my name with that of my friend, *"Elvis."*

A case in point!

During my years with Elvis, it was his habit, when at home in Memphis, to make Thursday nights his movie night. Every Thursday night we all found ourselves at the *"Memphian Theater"* enjoying a movie of Elvis' choice. It was usually very late because he would rent the entire facility after their normal hours of operation.

On one particular occasion, I had been away from the *"Graceland"* mansion since dark and in the pursuit of my *"own"* personal pleasures, I had lost track of the time. I suddenly noticed that it was past the time I was supposed to meet the guys for our scheduled trip to the Memphian Theatre.

After assuring myself that I was *"totally irresponsible,"* I asked myself, *"Now what 'cha gonna do?"* and immediately thereafter, I said to me, *"Me, you better 'git there as quick as ya can!"* So, I picked up a phone, near at hand, and called for a taxi.

Upon entering my *"black and white checkered"* chariot, I promised the driver a *"fifty dollar"* tip if he could make the thirty minute trip in fifteen minutes or less and then I sat back to watch the cars and streetlights go whisking by my window.

In just a little over fifteen minutes, I was stepping from my extremely swift and *"expensive"* ride and walking toward the front entrance to the Memphian. To my amazement, when I reached the front door, it was locked and I couldn't get in. That locked door really irritated me. After all, I was *"Donnie Sumner"* and I wanted in and I wanted in *"now!"*

During the major part of my years in the entertainment world, and then greatly escalating after joining the Elvis entourage, I had a tremendously over exaggerated opinion of my own self-worth. In those days, should one have occasion to open a dictionary to the word *"ego,"* they would have immediately observed my picture beside its definition.

Realizing that I, *"Donnie Sumner,"* was being denied entrance by reason of a locked door and still highly excited by the wild ride I had just experienced, I started banging as loudly as I could on the door that stood in my way.

Previously that evening, I had really been *"off duty"* and was quite disheveled to say the least.

Standing there hammering on the door, dressed in *"less than stylish attire,"* with my very long hair going in every direction and hollering, *"Let me in,"* it's no wonder that when an employee of the Memphian finally came to the door, opened it up and saw me, he angrily said to me, *"What 'cha' want?"*

I started briskly pushing him aside and angrily said, *"In and now!"* His response was to grab me by the arm and quickly assure me that my presence was not desired. Very gruffly he said to me, *"You can't come in here. We're closed and having a private viewing."* At that point, anyone with any intelligence at all would have stopped due to the fact that the *"grabber"* was approximately twice the size of the *"grabbee."* But *"not Ol' Donnie!"* ... *"Donnie Sumner"* didn't have to take that, off nobody!

I reached up with my free arm and gave the gentleman a very firm shove and then I quickly reached into my shirt to grab the medallion that hung from a chain around my neck. I pulled it out and stuck my *"TCB"* up in the air, like it was a cross holding back a vampire and then I defiantly hollered out, *"Back off dude! I'm with the 'PRESLEY' party!"* Bless his heart! It was  like someone had poured a bucket of cold water over his head. He stopped in his tracks and politely said to me, *"I'm sorry, Sir! I didn't know!"*

"It's all in the name!"

On another occasion, we were in Las Vegas, Nevada, a few days prior to Elvis' opening at the Hilton Hotel. That same week, *"Tom Jones"* was the main act at Caesar's Palace, just a short way from the Hilton and regardless of common belief, Tom and Elvis were *"very good friends"* and had great times together.

 We had been in rehearsal all afternoon preparing for our up-coming opening night. When the session concluded, I assumed that we were through until late that night when we were to assemble again in Elvis' suite but when Elvis got back to his suite there was nothing for him to do so he decided to go see the *"Tom Jones Show"* and when Elvis parties, *"everybody"* parties!

"Joe Espisito," Elvis' road manager, called the guys and told them that everyone was going to Caesar's Palace to see the Tom Jones show and when he called me, I told him that I didn't particular want to leave at the moment, so, I would catch a cab and be over there in a little bit. In a short time, I was ready to make my departure and I went downstairs at the Hilton and had the doorman hail me a taxi.

As soon as I arrived at Caesar's, I headed directly to the entrance of the showroom lounge. When I got there, a long line of people were waiting to be seated and like most patrons of the Vegas shows during that time period, they were all dressed in their finest apparel.

My attire was somewhat different than theirs. Never-the-less, dressed in a tank top shirt, blue jeans and Indian moccasins, I proceeded to make my way to the front of the line.

I finally found myself at the very head of the line, standing in front of two golden standards between which a wide purple rope was hanging and of course, *"it was in my way."*

As I reached down to unhook the small golden latch that held the rope to the standard, I felt a hand on my hand. I looked up and it was the hand of a short, stout Maitreya-de, dressed in a black tuxedo. As our eyes met he spoke to me in a distinct foreign accent and he said, *"Sorry, sir! We have a 'dress code' here and even if you were properly attired you must 'wait in line'!"*

Without a hint of a smile I said, *"Negatory man! I'm with the 'PRESLEY' party!"*

I find it amusing now but at the time, it did not strike me as funny when the Maitreya-de responded, *"Yes sir! I'm sure and my sister is his wife."* I immediately reached down into my tank top and arrogantly retrieved my magical *"TCB."* I leaned forward as far as I could and held it defiantly right in front of his face and loudly said, *"Does your sister have one of these?"* He smiled slightly and said, *"Pardon me sir! Follow me!"*

It really is *"all in the name."*

Time and events have changed my lifestyle since those times and I have become less Hilton and Caesar's oriented and have evolved into a more than frequent patron of a Waffle House or an Interstate truck stop and I am certain that if I stood sometime and said, *"Hi y'all! I'm Donnie!"* they would say *"Donnie who?"*

On the other hand, can you imagine what their reaction would be, if by some miracle, a handsome *"rock and roller"* were to walk in and announce, *"Hi! I'm Elvis!"*

"Elvis!" Now, that's a name!

- Donnie Sumner

A Good Name
is like a glass of water

The CLEANER it is
The BETTER it is

Gunfight At The E.P. Corral

*H*ave you ever died? I did once. At least, I thought I did!

Elvis loved to play practical jokes on his friends and he sure did a number on me once.

I was with The Stamps Quartet and we were enjoying our second engagement in Las Vegas with Elvis.

One morning about half way through the stay, *"Sonny West,"* the head of Elvis' security at the time, called my uncle J.D. and said he wanted the Stamps to come join in a special security meeting prior to our first performance that evening.

When we all got to the meeting, Sonny announced that they had received an anonymous note from an irate fan stating that he was *"gonna take Elvis down that night."*

Sonny gave each of us a personal assignment for the two shows we were to do that night. Each of us was given a particular section of the showroom to watch and if any male person moved in a suspicious manner during either show, we were to shout out to Sonny or Red and point to the person in question.

To my relief, nothing happened during the first performance but I was definitely not looking forward to the second show.

I had just returned to my room, after the first show, when Sonny called again and said it was imperative that we all get together. I hurriedly proceeded to join the others in Elvis' suite.

Once assembled, Sonny again took charge and he showed us all another note from the *"alleged perpetrator"* stating that Elvis would be *"dead before morning."*

"Red West" then took the lead and began briefing us on a new seating arrangement that would have us encircling Elvis on stage. We were also told to surround Elvis on all sides in transit to and from the showroom.

Unnoticed during the briefing, Sonny had left the suite, changed clothes and was about to put the *"icing on the cake"* that Elvis had prepared for us.

Elvis' suite was very large and included four bedrooms, three bathrooms, a kitchen, a dining room and an extremely large living room full of couches and plush chairs. When you entered the suite through its ornately carved wooden doors, you would notice a short hall, angling backward on the left side of the suite entrance. A full wet bar was against the left wall just  past this hallway entrance. Behind that wall was the dining room and it opened up into the living room at the far end of the bar.

At some point, during the time we all stood huddled together in the living room with Red holding our undivided attention, Sonny had quietly exited the suite and had re-entered through the housekeeper's entrance. As Red continued with our briefing session, Sonny came slipping down the foyer hall dressed in black pants, black shirt and a black velvet jacket. In addition to the all-black ensemble Sonny had also covered his entire head with a black ski mask.

To our sudden surprise, we heard a voice scream, *"Elvis, take this!"*

The outburst was immediately followed by the extremely loud sound of three or four shots being fired from a handgun that the assassin was holding.

At the sound of the shots, Elvis and one of the hotel security guards, fell face down onto the floor as though they were mortally wounded. Red grabbed his stomach and fell down, in like manner.

As soon as Elvis fell to the floor, my uncle *"J.D. Sumner,"* a World War II veteran, immediately jumped on top of Elvis, covering his entire body with his own and just lay there. Elvis never forgot that J.D., unaware

that he was being tricked, had put his own life on the line for him. The bond that was forged that night would never on this earth be broken.

When I heard shooting my first reaction was to get behind the bar as quickly as humanly possible. Two giant steps and a big leap propelled me over the bar. Feeling safe behind the bar, I squatted down, looking along the wall toward the entrance to the dining room.

The other members of the Stamps were having their own traumatic moments. *"Bill Baize,"* our tenor singer and *"Richard Sterban,"* our bass singer, had both found refuge behind a long coach in the living room.

When Red West had fallen down from the fake gunshot wound, his *"loaded"* pistol had slipped from his shoulder holster and had landed several inches from his body. Ed Enoch, our baritone singer and a Vietnam veteran, was feeling heroic, I suppose. He began crawling over toward Red's pistol laying on the living room floor. In the words of Red, ***"It's hard to play dead and, at the same time, try to keep somebody from gettin' their hands on a gun with 'live ammo'!"***

While all of us were ***"duckin' and hidin'"*** Sonny had sneaked ***"unseen"*** through the dining room that lay behind the bar wall and was on his way into the living room at the bars far end, for one ***"fake, final attempt."***

As I sat there hiding behind the bar, I saw a pistol slowly start to appear at the far end of the wall to my left. When the pistol finally came into full view, I realized it was being held by the ***"unknown assassin."*** Frightened to the point of nausea, I tried to find something I could use for a weapon. The only things under the counter were several large cans of tomato juice and orange juice. With nothing else at my disposal and with ***"my death imminent,"*** I grabbed a can of tomato juice with the intention of throwing it, as hard as I could, at the pistol I was looking at.

As soon as the can left my hand I knew that it was gonna miss the gun by a country mile and without losing my momentum, I jumped up, kept movin' forward and reached out to grab the gun. Rather than the gun, I grabbed Sonny's slippery velvet jacket and the intensity of my momentum caused my hands to slide completely free of the sleeve and I fell backward onto the floor.

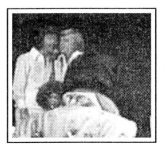

That's when Sonny put the barrel of his pistol to my forehead and hollered, ***"You're dead!"***

I might as well have been! I passed out colder than the proverbial cucumber. I don't know how long it took but when I opened my eyes, the first things I saw were Sonny, dressed in all black and Elvis, ***"laughing as hard as I had ever seen him laugh."***

Needless to say, I did the second show that night with a queasy stomach but nothing really mattered except the fact that:

"Elvis and I were both alive!"

- Donnie Sumner

Bravery is:

"Doing All You Can"

When:

"THERE'S NOTHING LEFT
FOR YOU TO DO"

I Ain't Gonna Miss Heaven

*"**I** ain't gonna miss Heaven on no technicality!"*

That was Elvis' reply to a humorous question *"Sammy Davis, Jr."* once asked.

During one of our Elvis shows at the old Hilton in Las Vegas, Sammy Davis, Jr, *"a great friend"* of Elvis', was invited to come enjoy our show as Elvis' special guest.

"The King" was in rare form that night and as usual, when a famous celebrity was in the audience, Elvis really *"showed off"* with all of the musical and stage skills he had so ably mastered.

After the show, all of us, along with Sammy Davis, Jr., went up to Elvis' suite on the top floor of the Hilton.

When we all got to the suite, Elvis was in the living room dressed in a blue suede ensemble, sporting an *"Elvis style,"* open collar, fancy white shirt.

Extremely visible, around Elvis' neck, were *"three"* elegant gold necklaces, each set with a precious stone of various kinds. Elvis always wore lots of jewelry but the thing that made these necklaces so noticeable was the fact that each of them was a *"religious symbol"* representing *"eternal life."*

Egyptian   Christian   Oriental

When we came in, Elvis stood up and with a big smile on his face, yelled, *"Great show guys! Thanks!"* He then walked over to Sammy Davis, shook his hand, hugged him and said, *"Thanks, man, for coming to the show."* Sammy responded with,

"It was a tremendous show, 'Mr. T.'!"

Elvis jokingly said, *"What's with the 'Mr. T.' stuff?"* To which Sammy answered, *"I wear necklaces but not three at a time." ... Why three?"* Elvis began to explain to Sammy that they were religious symbols and went on to share with him that they each symbolized eternal life. Sammy Davis said, *"You know I'm Jewish and I think you should have the 'Jewish' symbol too."* Elvis jokingly said, *"Buy me one and I'll wear it too!"* That's when Elvis made his memorable quote:

"I ain't gonna miss Heaven on no technicality!"

A few nights later, Sammy Davis came over to Elvis' suite after his own show and I saw him give Elvis a little box. When Elvis opened it, inside was a 14K gold *"Jewish symbol"* for eternal life embellished with a beautiful diamond. I heard Sammy say, *"I thought 'the diamond' might go good with 'the pearly gates'!"* To which they both shared a hearty laugh.

Jewish

Overwhelmingly, the question I am most frequently asked about my friend, Elvis is this: *"Was Elvis a Christian?"*

I generally answer that question with: *"None of us have the knowledge of God. Therefore, no one has the duty, the right nor the luxury to answer such a question and I truly do not know. That's between him and a higher power."*

I frequently continue with, *"A black minister in Mississippi publicly declared that he had the opportunity to baptize Elvis. The renowned evangelist, Rex Humbard, once stated that he was able to pray with Elvis prior to his death. I choose to take these gentlemen at their word."*

I always close my answer with:

*"I know that 'I am'
and I expectantly look forward
to seeing Elvis again."*

"SOMEDAY!"

- Donnie Sumner

You can't rewrite history
but:

The Future
Is Yet To Be Penned

Throw Him Back

"Heck! It's only Charlie!"

That's probably what the fans at the front of the stage thought when *"Charlie Hodge,"* Elvis' stage companion, landed in their arms.

In 1972, while on tour with Elvis, we did a performance at the coliseum in Hampton Roads, Virginia, near Norfolk, Virginia. That night, during the show, I witnessed one of the strangest and most humorous events that I ever experienced on an *"Elvis stage."*

The fans were especially active that night. In addition to the overly excited crowd, the stage set up was rather unusual for an *"Elvis concert."*

"Colonel Parker" was known for his carefully detailed preparations for all Elvis events but for some unknown reason: upon arrival at the venue, we noticed that the stage was about three to four feet higher than normal. When a person of average height was standing

at the front of the coliseum stage, their eye level was below the flooring of the stage and if they were unfortunate enough to be pressed up

against the stage front, all they would be able to see were the stage curtains covering its front.

For my first three or four tours with Elvis, the *"T.C.B. Band"* and *"Charlie Hodge"* had worn elaborately fringed western shirts as their stage apparel. For this particular tour, Elvis had *"Bill Belew,"* his personal stage wardrobe designer, to create uniforms for Charlie to match the basic format and color of the suits that he, himself, would be wearing on the tour.

On this particular night, Elvis was wearing a *"brand new, dazzling red outfit."* All during the show, Charlie was constantly by his side dressed in the *"matching red suit"* that Elvis had created for him.

During the night's events, I had no difficulty at all *"distinguishing between Elvis and Charlie"* but *"some folks did!"*

"Colonel Parker" Elvis' manager, always encouraged him to interact with the fans during the shows and as usual; all night, Elvis was constantly throwing scarves, kissing girls and touching hands as he vigorously performed his magic.

The concert was a great one and all was going well until close to the end of Elvis' performance. As he was nearing the close of his show that night, Elvis walked to the front of the *"very high"* stage; got down on both knees and was preparing to *"lean over the edge to kiss a girl."* Because he would had to kneel in such an unbalanced position, before Elvis knelt to reach down from the stage, *"Charlie Hodge,"* his stage companion, had knelt down first and had stuck out his extended arm past the front of the stage for Elvis to hold onto.

In their frenzy to touch Elvis: As soon as Charlie's *"rhinestoned and studded"* red sleeve cleared the edge of the stage, one or more of the excited fans reached up and pulled Charlie completely off of the stage, into their waiting arms.

On stage, I was seated behind The Sweet Inspirations and Kathy Westmoreland and from *"my"* vantage point, I wasn't exactly sure what had just happened to Charlie and my first thought was, *"Oh, Lord! Charlie just fell off of the stage and this puppy's high!"*

I was sitting there concerned about his well-being when, all of a sudden, I saw Charlie come sailing back onto the stage.

I wasn't in the crowd at the front of the stage but in my imagination, I sometimes hear them saying, *"Aw shucks! This ain't Elvis! Let's throw him back!"*

Once Charlie had safely landed back onto the stage and after he had regained his composure; he stood up, pushed his guitar around to hang on his back, spread his arms real wide and leaned over into a deep bowing position and in a voice mimicking that of Elvis, said, *"Thank you very much Ladies and Gentlemen!"*

On numerous occasions before his passing, I heard Elvis tell various friends about Hampton Roads, Virginia and *"the night they threw Charlie back on the stage!"* When Charlie was present during Elvis' telling of the story, *"he would laugh harder than anyone else."*

If Charlie were still here to read what I have just written especially for you:

He Would Laugh Again!

- Donnie Sumner

He Who
Laughs At Himself
will invariably have
THE BEST LAUGH

Panties In Bloom

*H*ave you ever seen a tree, full of *"multi-colored panties?"*

"I have!"

Anyone fortunate enough to have attended an Elvis concert will attest to the fact that, during the show, there would be numerous articles thrown onto the stage by excited fans.

Charlie Hodge was Elvis' faithful stage companion and it was part of his responsi-bility to follow Elvis  around and pick up the articles that were thrown onto the stage in order to make Elvis' paths safe during the performance. By the time any given show had ended, Charlie would always have an entire box full of room keys, stuffed animals, flowers and notes along with an assortment of other articles. I was often amazed at some of the *"unusual gifts"* that were thrown at Elvis' feet.

The most frequently noticed *"offerings"* were ladies panties and Elvis always created a very noticeable moment when a pair came flying in his direction. He would often pick them up, point to some good looking lady in the audience and say, *"Honey, did 'you' lose these?"* Regardless of the comment he would make, the audience always found it extremely funny. *"Me too!"*

What the fans didn't understand was this: For the most part, these incidents were planned by Colonel Tom Parker, Elvis' manager. During each performance, the Colonel would select some *"lady"* fan, walk up behind her, hand her a pair of panties, escort her toward the stage and then tell her to, *"Throw 'em at Elvis."* Of course, the sweet fans he selected were always overjoyed at the opportunity and they always, *"gladly,"* granted the Colonel's request.

On a number of occasions, there would be the presentation of a *"legitimate"* pair of undergarments and in order to plan for this, the Colonel had informed Elvis that any garment still bearing the price tag would be from him. Knowing which articles he could use, Elvis soon developed the habit of walking over to *"J. D. Sumner of The Stamps*

Quartet," spreading the waist band and slipping the garment down over J.D.'s head with J.D.'s ears stickin' out through the leg openings and even though I witnessed the scene on multiplied occasions, it never ceased to be extremely funny.

J.D. was a serious collector of *"Elvis memorabilia"* and would invariably save anything that came his way during an Elvis performance. Consequently, within a short time, J.D. had acquired a *"large size"* container, full of *"ladies panties!"*

With my *"Uncle J.D."* on the road for long periods of time, my *"Aunt Mary,"* J.D.'s wife, filled a lot of her time making scrapbooks and other displays of paraphenallia that J.D. had collected. She found Uncle Jake's *"panty collection"* extremely interesting and very humorous.

The best I can recall at this point, it was in the fall of 1974 and all the Elvis entourage was on the road and while we were all away, Aunt Mary had decided to buy some new chairs for J.D.'s *"man cave."* During her *"hunting expedition"* she discovered a room ornament that caught her attention. It was a barren tree, standing about five feet tall, with wide, bare branches and secured in a beautiful gold-plated plant receptacle. As soon as she saw it, she had an amazingly creative idea. She purchased the piece and had it delivered. When it was finally delivered, she had the delivery men to set it up in Uncle Jake's private den.

When we returned from our engagement with Elvis, J.D. went to his condo, walked in, threw down his luggage, kissed Aunt Mary and then, together, they proceeded toward Uncle Jake's hide-away in order for him to unload his new *"stage memories."*

Many times I heard Aunt Mary's *"personal narrative"* of the moment and she would always say, *"When J.D. walked in and saw that tree filled with panties, he stepped back and said, 'My God! They're alive'!"*

A few years later, my Aunt Mary received her gift of *"eternal life."* Following her *"home-going,"* I would, very often, go over and visit Uncle Jake in order to see if there was anything he needed or if there was anything I could do to make his life more enjoyable.

At some point during each visit, we would invariably find ourselves seated in the big leather chairs in his den. Sometimes we made jokes, often

we sang and frequently, we just sat together, each of us savoring in our private thoughts, During these *"quiet moments,"* I would often glance over toward, Uncle Jake and each time that I did, I observed him silently staring at the *"panty tree"* Aunt Mary had

made for him. Since that time, Uncle Jake has also *"left the building"* to be forever reunited with his sweetheart. In the days that have followed his departure, I have often pondered at what might have been Uncle Jake's thoughts when he would sit with me and quietly view his *"panty tree."* I guess I'll never know but I can certainly assure myself that whatever they were, they were filled with *"loving memories."*

To the best of my knowledge, J.D.'s daughters, Shirley and Frances, have safely secured all of Uncle Jake's personal artifacts in a safe and well maintained storage facility. I have never met the attendant in charge of servicing the facility but I like to imagine that the first time he opened the door to Uncle Jake's unit and looked in, he said to himself, *"My Lord! There's a tree growing 'panties'! I wonder where in the world that 'botanical wonder' came from?"* I have never been afforded the privilege of meeting that particular gentleman and he doesn't know me but I can positively answer his question:

It was made by: *"My Aunt Marty"* for: *"My Uncle Jake"*

From Panties ... Elvis Gave To J.D.

- Donnie Sumner

People and Things may fade from view but:

Memories Always Remain

and

"Love Lasts Forever"

Elvis And The Living Room Quartet

*E*veryone has one or more unfulfilled dreams.

Elvis was no exception and one of his life-long desires was to be in a *"Gospel Quartet."*

I love *"Gospel Quartet music"* with a passion and have been a professional member of that musical community for over a half century but *"my"* love for that genre was superseded by that of my friend, *"Elvis."*

In 1954, a Memphis based Gospel Quartet known as, *"The Songfellows,"* had an opening available in their group for a *"baritone"* singer. Motivated by his love for *"Gospel"* music and now having an opportunity to realize his ambition, Elvis *"auditioned"* for the position. Much to the group manager's *"later dismay,"* Elvis was not accepted by The Songfellows.

It has been stated that *"What goes around, comes around"* and in this particular instance, it definitely came around and may I add, *"swiftly."* Within a few days, after the groups' rejection of Elvis, he signed a contract with *"Sun Records,"* owned by *"Sam Phillips"* and *"the rest is history!"* In all probability, the gentleman in The Songfellows Quartet that refused to give Elvis a job has wished, *"many times,"* that he had made a *"wiser"* decision.

It was a *"long time coming"* but Elvis eventually got to sing in a *"quartet."* Two of them as a matter of fact!

I once asked Elvis how his love for Gospel music was born. He relayed to me how, as a *"little guy,"* he used sit outside a small church in Tupelo, Mississippi and listen to its black congregation sing during their revival meetings. I found it humorous when he told me that, *"there was one dear sister in that church that had more moves that me!"*

A lot of what became *"Elvis' style"* came from *"black Gospel"* and *"southern Gospel."* The groups that most influenced the music of Elvis were *"The Golden Gate Quartet" "The Blackwood*

Brothers Quartet" and *"The Statesmen Quartet."* According to what Elvis told me, he always wanted to sing *"the loud high notes"* like *"James Blackwood."* On one occasion, I asked Elvis where he got his *"iconic leg"* idea. In paraphrase, this was his story: ***"Right after Colonel Parker took me on, he told me I needed to 'move more' and 'dancin' ain't my thing' so I tried to work on something else. I always loved The Statesmen Quartet, especially the bass singer, 'Big Chief' Wetherington. When The Statesmen would sing a fast song, Ol' Chief would turn sideways, stick out one leg and start to move it all kinds of ways, in rhythm to the music. When I started trying to get 'me' some 'moves,' I remembered watching Chief and I thought I would give it a whirl. I guess it worked. At least it did 'until' I got on 'The Ed Sullivan Show'!"***

All of the fast Gospel spirituals that Elvis recorded came directly from the music of *"The Golden Gate Quartet."* Elvis listened to their records constantly and his versions of *"I John,"* *"Run On,"* and *"Swing Down Chariot,"* are exact duplicates of their renditions. Elvis knew every unique *"hot lick"* and *"inflection"* that The Golden Gate group had recorded and he performed their songs with perfection.

Charlie Hodge, Elvis' closest friend, was *"keeper of the records."* and Charlie had designed a *"custom made"* case in which he secured all of Elvis' Gospel records. Everywhere Elvis went, Charlie was always right there as his faithful companion and he always carried with him, Elvis' Gospel recording collection and a portable record player. Shortly before Charlie *"left the building,"* I borrowed Elvis' Gospel records from him. Charlie had meticulously cared for them and they were all in excellent condition. I transferred them all to my computer and I have often listened to them. On each occasion, I recall fond memories of sitting with Elvis as he listened intently to the music and in my imagination, I can almost hear him singing along.

Included in the list of Elvis' favorite Gospel Quartets was the group, *"J.D. Sumner and The Stamps Quartet."* For eight years I was the lead singer for The Stamps and enjoyed to pleasure of singing with *"My Uncle J.D."* who was my life-long, musical hero. As part of the *"The Stamps,"* I had the fortunate opportunity to join Elvis in 1971. *"The Stamps,"* along with *"The Sweet Inspirations"* and *"Kathy Westmoreland"* sang as Elvis' backup ensemble on stage and on his recordings.

During Elvis' stage appearances, as part of his vocal ensemble, I was frequently called upon to hit Elvis' last *"big high note"* for him on a given song. It was not because he couldn't hit the note, it was simply because *"he didn't want to."* Very frequently we would come to the big finale of a production number and Elvis would point to me. When he did, I knew I was supposed to sing his note so he could interact with a fan or do an impressive karate kata of some sort.

Late in 1973, I left The Stamps and organized my own group. I named my group, *"The Tennessee Rangers"* and  shortly after The Rangers came into existence, I got a call from *"Charlie Hodge"* who informed me that Elvis wanted my group to come to Vegas for a few days. Charlie went on to explain that Elvis wanted *"me"* to do the *"high notes"* for his friend, *"Tom Jones"* who was having throat problems. Vegas is very dry and unless you take special precautions, your voice will become very raspy and you will experience what the singers there refer to as, *"Vegas throat."* I readily accepted Charlie's invitation *and* he made the necessary travel arrangements. Soon thereafter, *"Sherril 'Shaun' Nielsen, Tim Baty* and *myself"* were en route to Las Vegas, *"aboard Elvis' private jet."*

For the next few days, three Gospel hillbillies got to play *"star,"* courtesy of our friend, *"Elvis."*

The next weekend, both *"Elvis"* and *"Tom Jones"* ended their engagements and Elvis hosted a closing night party in his suite at the Hilton Hotel. As Elvis' guests, The Rangers were included in the VIP list.

Our late night had swiftly become early morning when I heard, *"Hey Donnie!"* I recognized Elvis' voice and I responded with, *"Yes, Sir!"* I went over to where Elvis was and he said, *"You remember that song, 'In The Sweet Bye and Bye' that you sang with The Stamps?"* I answered him, *"Yes, Sir!"* Elvis smiled at me and said, *"How 'bout singing it for me."* When Elvis smiles at you and asks you for a favor, *"how can you refuse?"* So, I said, *"Sure!"* and called for Shaun and Tim to join me. We then got around Elvis' piano and began to sing.

Soon after we finished the song, Elvis went into his bedroom. In just a bit, he came back into the living room, walked up to me, handed me a piece of bathroom tissue with some writing on it and said, *"Check this out and tell me what 'cha think!"*

I took the lengthy piece of tissue and began to read. It said, *"I, Elvis Aaron Presley, agree to pay to Donnie Sumner, Shaun Nielsen and Tim Baty, over the next twelve months, the sum total of XXXX dollars for their full time services, to sing at my request, 'In The Sweet Bye and Bye'."*

Once my eyes uncrossed, I said, *"Are you kiddin' me?"* Elvis said, *"No man! Y'all wanna be 'my' quartet?"* After a *"split second"* of deliberation, I said, *"You bet 'cha!"*

After the three of us had scribbled our signatures on the document, Elvis walked over to his Dad, Mr. Vernon Presley, and said, *"Well, Daddy, I finally got in 'a quartet!"* I have often wondered why he used the word *"finally"* in as-much-as he had already made a *"world famous"* record as part of *"The Million Dollar Quartet."*

The following week, Elvis took us all to his Hollywood home and shortly after our arrival there, *"Larry Geller,"* one of Elvis' close friends, came by the house to show Elvis his new book that had just been released entitled, *"The Voice."* Larry's book had a beautiful cover and after admiring the artwork a while, Elvis said, *"Donnie, y'all ain't The Rangers no more! From now on y'all are, 'Voice'!"*

Every night thereafter, until September of 1976, at some point during the evening we found ourselves around the piano singing old, slow gospel tunes for Elvis, as he would request them. Without exception, every sing-a-long included, *"In The Sweet Bye and Bye."* I recall one night when we sang the song *"eighteen"* times, back to back, all four verses. That friend, is a lot of *"sweet bye byes!"*

Yes sir! I've sung a lot of *"Gospel songs"* with a *"lot of people"* but some of my fondest memories were created in *"Elvis' living room,"* around *"his piano,"* the *"four"* of us singing *"together"* as:

"Elvis and The Living Room Quartet!"

- Donnie Sumner

A Song A Day
Keeps The Blues Away
Sing Often ... Sing Loud ... Be Happy

The Spot

I am no Rembrandt but I enjoy trying my hand at oil painting.

My brother, Dr. F.L. Sumner is the true artist in our family. His paintings can be seen in galleries and homes in multiplied places. The only available viewing of my renderings can be seen only in the privacy of my own *"man cave."* I am much more well known for my musical skills than for my artistic abilities. At this point in my life, I don't have nearly as much spare time to smear paint on a canvas as I did during the time I was living and touring with my friend, *"Elvis!'*

Back in those days, life on the road was a *"piece of cake!"* The only responsibilities I had were eating, dressing, singing and having fun. It seemed that everything else in my daily routine was taken care of by someone else.

If you enjoy traveling in luxury, I sure wish that you too had been afforded the opportunity to travel with the *"Elvis entourage!"*

Our daily routine was to pack our main luggage just before retiring for the night and set the pieces outside our room door. We always had a secure floor and felt at ease regarding the safety of our luggage. Each of us had a small shoulder bag in which we would carry a few personal items but everything else went out into the hall. During the night the luggage crew would come to each door, pick up the pieces and put them on the plane that was awaiting us for our next day's flight.

If you were a lover of breakfast, when you woke up you could call room service and then enjoy a fine breakfast, *"compliments of Elvis."* When the scheduled departure time rolled around, we would all meet in the hotel lobby, then get aboard our bus, travel to our plane and head toward the next venue.

Once we landed in the next city, everything was in reverse. We disembarked, rode the bus to our hotel, went to our rooms and entered, using the key that each of had received during the bus transit. When we entered our individual rooms, the amenity that awaited us was the *"sweetest part of the whole cake."* Our stage clothes would be neatly hanging in the closet and regardless of how many bags you had, they were all conveniently located around the room. I assure you that I miss that particular detail in my travels these days. When I check in now-a-days,

I am carrying everything except the *"kitchen sink"* and sometimes I remind myself of a homeless person pushing a shopping cart full of collected treasures.

By the time we got everything squared away in our room, it was usually time for lunch. So, *"call room service"* and enjoy another meal compliments of *"The Boss!"* After eating, some of the boys and girls would take a quick nap. Others were like me and would run from one room to another stirring up excitement. If I had taken more naps during those days, in all probability, I would not require as many as I find necessary now, in my *"older years."*

The only thing left to do was get dressed, travel to the concert venue, *"oom-pa-pa and scoobie-do-wah"* a little, come back to the hotel, party a little, pack your luggage, set it all outside your door and prepare to start the same schedule again tomorrow.

In-as-much as I could travel with all the luggage I wanted to with no strain on *"my"* back, I developed a habit that I stuck to until my final tour with Elvis.

I had one suitcase that was custom built for me. I referred to it as my *"party bag!"* Inside the bag I carried a full supply of snacks, paper party bowls, napkins, six tall candles, a six foot by six foot fish net and a  small bag full of decorative items for the fish net. Also included in the party bag was a goodly supply of five by seven inch art canvases; along with a full complement of oil paints, brushes and painting knives. My first duty when I got to my room each day, was to unpack the party bag and place all the items in their places. I always hung the fish net across the ceiling and put all the little frills in it. When I was finished, it would look like *"happy hour"* at a political convention.

It seemed that the rooms of *"J.D. Sumner" "Glen D. Hardin"* and myself were the ones that could always be found with a gathering of show personnel and I had a personal requirement for anyone who came to my room and stayed any length of time. Before they could leave, they had to go over to the paint table, pick up a canvas and paint a picture. During the course of my travels with Elvis I have seen some of the weirdest and ugliest *"star prints"* one can imagine. I collected a lot of canvases.

Somewhere, amid all the confusion of an unpleasant divorce in 1979, all of my friend's paintings were lost and I regret it to this day. I am especially troubled by the loss of one in particular.

On March 21, 1976, Elvis was playing Cincinnati, Ohio and the entire cast was staying at the Carousel Inn. I had checked in, arranged my room and was preparing to go visit the room of my Uncle, *"J.D. Sumner," "The World's Lowest Bass Voice."* As I was *gittin'* it all together, I heard a knock on my door. When I opened  the door, there stood *"Red West,"* one of Elvis' bodyguards and *"My Friend, Elvis!"* I invited them in and after a few remarks, Elvis began to tell me that his Dad, *"Vernon Presley,"* would be celebrating a birthday on April 10 and that He wanted my group *"Voice Inc."* to do a little concert for the birthday party he was planning for Vernon. Of course, I did exactly as you would have done. I said, *"O.K.!"*

We continued talking for a while and as Elvis was starting to leave, I said to him, *"Nobody leaves my room until they paint a picture."* He responded with *"What do you mean?"* I showed him the paints and canvases and said back to him, *"Paint me a picture."* After saying to me, *"I ain't never painted nothin' in my life 'cept my girlfriend's fingernails in high school,"* Elvis picked up a brush, dabbed it with some black paint and then painted a small black blob on the top canvas. When he finished the black round circle he said with a smile, *"I'm gonna call it, 'THE SPOT!' Because your room is definitely 'the spot'!"*

I can still see him and hear him laughing as he left my room to head back to his own suite.

I have painted a few pictures in my time, some good and some not so good. I am not really interested in looking at my own paintings these days because, like me, they're *"gittin' old an wrinkled."*

It's not within my power to do so but *"if I could:"* I would unlock the archives of *"lost articles"* and retrieve some of my past treasures. If I were told that I could choose only *"one:"* I would choose a painting I once owned that had been rendered by a very close friend.

I would choose:
"The Spot" by "My Friend Elvis!"

- Donnie Sumner

Louie The Juggler

*E*lvis looked *"absolutely stunning"* in his stage wardrobe but I have never been able to say the same in regard to *"my own."*

During the time I sang lead for *"J.D. Sumner and The Stamps Quartet,"* our entire stage attire consisted of custom made *"two piece"* suits. Although the suits were designed in a conservative style, they were, often times, in flamboyant colors. I have

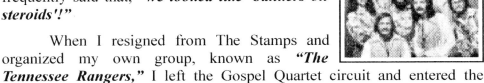

frequently said that, *"we looked like 'bankers on steroids'!"*

When I resigned from The Stamps and organized my own group, known as *"The Tennessee Rangers,"* I left the Gospel Quartet circuit and entered the genre of Country Music. The group soon became regulars on Nashville's *"Grand Ole Opry"* and that's when my wardrobe began to change.

Our Nashville tailor, *"Mr. G.,"* designed several outfits for The Rangers and each of them contained a generous supply of suede fringe. I can assure you that when we put those rascals on and walked onto a stage, we looked like the cast of some old cowboy movie. For some folks, the look may be a little out of the ordinary but as far as I was concerned, *"We didn't look too abnormal."*

In 1973, I woke up one morning in Hollywood, California and I was in the home of my new employer, *"Elvis Presley!"* Now that, boys and girls, was a *"mind blower!"* With the new job, I also embarked upon a transformation from *"country fringe"* to *"rock n' roll glitze!"*

Elvis had contracted, *"Sherrill 'Shaun' Nielsen"* *"Tim Baty"* and myself, to be his *"in-house singers."* Our main obligation was to sing *"Gospel Music"* to him, upon request. Every night, Elvis would have us sing song after song, sometimes until the wee hours of the morning. He would sit in a chair and call out the titles and we would sing what he had just asked for. I *"love"* Gospel Music but I have yet to meet anyone who was more obsessed with the genre than was my friend, *"Elvis!"*

One evening, shortly after Elvis hired The Rangers, we were in the den at his Hillcrest Drive estate. *"Larry Geller,"* a very close friend of

Elvis, had come over to show Elvis a copy of a new book he had written and one that had just been released. The volume was a study on meditation and its title read, *"The Voice."* Elvis examined the book and complimented Larry on his efforts. The book had elaborate art work on the cover and as Elvis intently examined the art he suddenly turned to me and said, *"Donnie, y'all aren't 'The Rangers' anymore. From now on, I'm gonna call ya 'Voice'!"* From that time forward we were introduced as *"Voice."*

I don't have the ability to express what a total joy it was living and working with *"My Friend Elvis."* I got to sing to more people, travel in more luxury and experience more fun, than I could have ever dreamed of.

One of my many experiences was the opportunity to be a part of *"The Jerry Lewis Labor Day Telethon."*

It was customary, during those years, for every hotel in Las Vegas to send a representative to the telethon along with a contribution payable to *"The Muscular Dystrophy Foundation."* Included in the list of benefactors was *"The Las Vegas Hilton Hotel."* In addition to the hotel gifts, it was not uncommon for some of the celebrities who were appearing at the various show rooms in Vegas to also make contributions. When a headliner made a gift of generous size they were asked to perform on the live broadcast. Among the names of those gracious patrons there was one that headed the list in total funds contributed: *"Elvis Presley!"* Although Elvis never performed on the telethon he was certainly one of its largest personal contributors.

I guess Elvis thought it would be great exposure for my group because for the next three years he sent us to the telethon as his representatives to present a very generous contribution. By reason of the names *"Elvis Presley"* and *"The Hilton Hotel"* along with the amount of *"Elvis' large gift;"* Voice had the privilege of singing on the telethon for three years and it was always an exciting and *"star studded"* event.

Just prior to the 1975 telethon, Elvis had designed a new jumpsuit for Voice and on Labor Day of that year we wore it at the Muscular Dystrophy gala.

I wish you could have seen those jump-suits. They were designed with all the *"Elvis amenities"* including flared and split trouser legs, hi-boy collars and some ruffles. The outfit was one piece with a side zipper and had shoulder straps and a sown-in shirt. The sown-in shirt had billowing sleeves, elastic bands at the wrist with ruffles extending from the wrist and covering about half of the hand. The final blow to the design was the color combination Elvis chose. The material was rendered in bright yellow knit material with the shirt and the trouser leg inlays made from material containing varying shades of brown, black and tan camouflage.

Elvis loved bananas and always had a supply available to him. He  was particularly fond of the *"Chiquita"* brand. In those days I stood six foot, four inches tall and weighed only one hundred and fifty pounds. I was so thin, *"Charlie Hodge,"* Elvis right-hand man, used to say that my *"pajamas only had one stripe."* I guess it was those two facts that prompted Elvis' step brother, *"Rickey Stanley,"* to say, the first time he saw me dressed in mine; *"You looked like a bruised banana!"* From that time forward, Ricky and his other two bro-thers, *"David"* and *"Billy,"* always called me by the nickname, *"Chiquita!"*

The final blow to *"Ole Chiquita"* occurred during the, above mentioned, 1975 Jerry Lewis telethon.

Shaun, Tim and I, along with a check from Elvis, were backstage at the Sahara Hotel in Las Vegas awaiting the time slot that had been allocated to Voice. It's difficult for me stand still when I'm waiting to go on stage and especially so when I'm donned in a bright yellow *"banana"* outfit. Due to the anxiety of the moment, I was aimlessly walking around backstage when, out of the darkness, a man came rushing toward me, grabbed my arm and began to pull me toward the stage wing. His only comment was, *"Hurry! You're on next!"* I've very conscientious in regard to show times and their time slots and I couldn't understand how I could be on next but in compliance with the floor director's insistent urging, I followed him to the stage wing. As I stood there listening to Jerry's introduction of the next act, it certainly didn't sound like it was gonna be Voice and furthermore, I couldn't see Shaun and Tim anywhere! With an air of uncertainty I turned to the floor director and said, *"Are you sure I'm on next!"* Apparently, he was not accustomed to being questioned because he responded with a brisk, *"Of course I am!"* He then pulled out a small flashlight, opened a printed schedule, shined his flashlight onto the schedule, pointed to a line on the schedule and said to me, *"See that! . . .*

Right There! . . . You're on next!"

The line read:
"LOUIE THE JUGGLER!"

My outfit may have been confusing but I *"did"* get on the show that night and it was not as *"Louie The Juggler!"*

During the passing of many years, I have been called by a lot of names including *"Chiquita"* and *"Louie The Juggler."* Those, along with any of the others that might have appeared on the list, are *"all"* perfectly O.K. with me as-long-as you follow it with the extension:

"A FRIEND OF ELVIS!"

- Donnie Sumner

The Name
by which you are called
is not really you!

Truly Know

Who and What You Are

and then

JUST BE

YOURSELF!

The Night Some Of Niagara Falls Fell

I never needed security guards but *"Elvis did!"*

I can stand in a crowd and never be touched by human hands but on the other-hand, *"Elvis was a different story."*

When in public view, Elvis drew fans toward him like a magnet. It was impossible for his fans to perceive him as a normal friend. He was a superstar and that was the manner in which he was viewed by all who came into an approachable distance to him. Consequently, he was crowded by fans trying to simply touch him or have a personal exchange with him. Often times in the frenzy, accidents were caused to happen and not too infrequently, bodily harm was inflicted upon a fan.

Although Elvis depended upon his security personnel for his own protection against harm from some irate individual, a great deal of their attention was devoted to providing a safe environment for the fans that would rush to be close to him.

"Sonny West, Red West and Dave Hebler," Elvis' lead bodyguards, were absolute masters in crowd control techniques and the art of providing courteous attention to the safety of Elvis' fans.

During the hundreds of shows that I did with Elvis, I witnessed a considerable number of instances that required the skills of Sonny, Red and Dave and they always came thru like the champs they were.

"Colonel Tom Parker," Elvis' manager, was also very active in the security details of our tours. The Colonel always utilized *"extra security"* from the local police force at each venue. He was always very generous with extra pay for the officers that attended to Elvis' security and in each city, he somehow developed a very close relationship with each individual force.

On a few occasions, the local security detail had their personal difficulties as well. I recall one such incident at the Elvis concert in Niagara Falls, New York on June 24, 1974. Elvis delivered two great performances that day, a matinee at 3 P.M. and then another at 8:30 P.M.

At one point during the evening performance, Elvis threw two handfuls of scarves into the audience. *"All at one time!"* As the scarves floated in the breeze and began falling into the audience, the excited crowd began rushing toward the stage like a rushing river trying to get over a small dam. As the local police officers  attempted to slow the advancing crowd, three of them were knocked to the ground and walked on by unobserving fans. They suffered various cuts and bruises along with a couple of sprained limbs.

Although she was not injured, a female officer, caught by the rush, was forced against the stage front and was being seriously pressed against it by the combined power of the frenzied crowd. As she stood their screaming for some help, *"Elvis, Charlie Hodge, Sonny West and Red West,"* all quickly ran to the front of the stage. They grabbed the arms of the lady officer in distress and lifted her up onto the stage. In all

 probability, she felt much better after Elvis had placed a scarf around her neck and *"kissed"* her. As soon as the lady officer returned to her post, some fan ran up to her, grabbed the scarf from around her neck and disappeared back into the crowd. Elvis with his *"always observing eyes"* saw what had happened and called the sweet little officer back onto the stage and thrilled her a *"second time"* with another kiss and another scarf. I'm certain that she is still enjoying each remembrance of her *"valor award"* as it was presented to her in 1974 by Elvis Presley.

The crowd was extremely active during that entire performance. It seemed like no one wanted to sit down. At any given time during the show, a large portion of the audience was in the standing mode.

In the center, near the front of audience, one particular robust lady must have thought that she was on *"American Bandstand,"* because all she wanted to do was *"boogie dance"* all thru the performance. With her constant screaming, standing and gyrations, she we blocking the view and diminishing the joy of other fans. After a lengthy period of patience, *"another lady officer"* in the local security detail attempted to persuade the dancing lady to have a seat. Her suggestion to the *"robust dancer"* was not accepted with grace. Being considerably larger than the police lady, the other woman chose to make a fist, draw back her arm and unexpectedly *"clobber"* the lady officer, knocking her to the ground. I am confident that the dear soul did not enjoy the *"dancing hall"* that was made available to her a little later by the *"Niagara Falls law enforcement personnel."*

Elvis had the unique ability of being able to create humor amid any unusual experience that might arise during one of his performances. When the offending lady was escorted from the venue, Elvis lay down on the stage to sing his next song. He told the audience that the lady had made him nervous and he was *"gonna have to take a rest."*

With a *"grateful heart"* and with his always *"generous spirit;"* after the show, Elvis personally saw to it that each of the five officers received a substantial gift for their *"active"* participation in his performance.

If I had known about the gift that was awaiting all the participants in the exciting events of that performance, I might have borrowed a badge from a nearby police officer, attached it to the front of my jump suit, jumped down off the stage, moved close to where Elvis was, slapped myself real hard and fallen face down onto the floor.

But the simple truth is, I never had to slap myself to be the recipient of Elvis' gracious attention because that's not what his friendship required.

Elvis was always giving,
always considerate,
always loyal
and shall remain:
Always in my thoughts.

- Donnie Sumner

When you dress for the day,
Don't forget to:
Slip On A Little Courtesy.

Elvis The "Sleepy-Head" Songwriter

*"**W**here did all you guys sleep!"*

That seems like a reasonable question that one would ask and it has been posed to me on many occasions.

There are several of us guys that still speak about *"living with Elvis."* Anyone that has seen Elvis' *"Graceland Mansion"* would definitely know that there could not possibly have been that many bedrooms inside the structure.

So, the question : *"If you lived with Elvis, where did you sleep!"*

First of all, *"living with Elvis"* meant that *"where ever Elvis was, you were there too."* The entire group of guys that Elvis called *"family"* were with him constantly and I do mean *"constantly!"* The last year I was with Elvis, I slept in my Nashville home only twelve nights. The remainder of the time I was in close proximity to *"my friend, Elvis."*

I have never known the luxury of being a *"superstar"* but during my association with Elvis, I came to know that *"seclusion"* is part of the life style and in your efforts to enjoy a relatively *"normal"* existence, it is not uncommon to frequently feel a sense of *"loneliness."*

I truly feel that Elvis avoided a lot of these moments by surrounding himself with his *"family"* of friends at all times. Every moment that Elvis was awake, he wanted all eighteen of us to be within eye sight. We watched a lot of television, told a lot of stories, discussed numerous books, made a lot of jokes and enjoyed a host of other exciting activities. I have often described it as, *"a teenage boys club living in a tree house!"*

At least one night a week, Elvis would rent the *"Memphian theatre"* where he once worked as an usher and the entire group would enjoy a night at the movies, watching a film that Elvis had personally requested.

It was not uncommon for Elvis to rent the entire *"Fairgrounds Amusement Park"* in Memphis and show up with all of us, as-well-as a host of invited guests. No one will ever again have the opportunity but in your imagination, should you ever decide to ride *"the bump cars"* or the *"double Ferris wheel"* with Elvis: *"Don't!"* Elvis loved both! When he was driving the bump cars, his goal was not winning a race. His objective

58

was to see how often he could knock you up against the railing and how hard he could make you hit. Personally, I don't like to get more than one foot off of the ground at any given time and I once made the mistake of riding the *"double Ferris wheel"* with Elvis and I sitting in the *"same seat."* I didn't know when the ride started that one of Elvis' thrills was riding the Ferris wheel until his seat was at the very top and then signaling the attendant to stop the ride. When my particular ride with Elvis stopped, I became as nervous as *"a long tailed cat in a room full of rocking chairs."* I really dislike heights! My *"fright"* became even more intense when Elvis started rocking the chair *"back and forth"* to see how much it would take to make me *"squeal!"* I can assure you that, *"I did!"* and might I add, *"like a stuck pig!"*

At the close of an *"Elvis' day,"* we all would head for our sleeping quarters and they were not at Graceland.

Elvis had two homes that we frequented. Graceland in Memphis and his last Hollywood home on Monovale Drive.

When in Hollywood, we stayed at The Holiday Inn on Interstate 5 and commuted to Elvis' home via the cars that Elvis had rented for each of us. Elvis had a year-round lease on the top floor of the hotel and each of us eighteen men had our own room that *"we"* called home.

When we were in Memphis, the same was true with The Howard Johnson facility that was just a few doors north of Graceland on Elvis Presley Boulevard. (*As a side-bar comment in regard to Elvis Presley Boulevard: Elvis said to me on one occasion,* **"I don't watch the Memphis news because I got nervous one time when they announced that, 'The body of middle aged woman was found on 'Elvis Presley' this morning'!"**)

The only ones of us that ever slept at Graceland were, *"Red West and Sonny West,"*

Elvis' bodyguards along with *"Charlie Hodge,"* Elvis' closest friend, and myself. Elvis wanted a bodyguard and a piano player at his *"beck and call"* at all times. Two of us were there each night and we took alternating evenings. Unless special arrangements had been made, we were paired together as *"Sonny and Charlie,"* *"Red and*

myself."

One evening in early in 1976, the day's activities had come to a close and Elvis had gone upstairs to his Graceland, *"fortress of solitude,"* Red and I, both songwriters, had taken the occasion of Elvis' early retiring as an opportunity to collaborate on the writing of a new song for Elvis.

We must have been singing and playing the living room piano rather loudly because Elvis apparently heard what we were doing be-cause he came downstairs. He was dressed in his pajamas and his hair was not as well groomed as it was always seen on stage: *"It was a mess!"*

As I look back on it now, I will state for the record that as he stood there on the staircase of Graceland in his pajamas and with his tussled hair, Elvis still looked *"grander"* than I could ever hope to look myself, under any condition.

In his hand was a torn piece of paper. Elvis came over to the piano and handed me the bit of paper and said, *"Y'all put me some music to these words!"* I took the note and Red responded with *"Will do boss!"* Elvis turned and walked back upstairs. When he was gone, Red and I began to examine the lyrics that Elvis had given us. The words had been written with a well used felt tip marker. In addition, Elvis had made the lines even wider by pressing down on the marker. Consequently, very few of the words were dicernable.

We tried diligently to decipher what Elvis had written but in the end we were unable to do so. Elvis never mentioned his poetic effort again and *"we"* certainly weren't gonna volunteer any information regarding our inept reading skills.

I still have the note tucked away in a picture album and have viewed it on past occasions. To this day, neither Red nor I have any idea as to what the true message of the offering was but *"whatever"* it was; I'm sure it would have been *"a hit"* because;

"Elvis Wrote It!"

- Donnie Sumner

A man isn't poor
As Long As He Can Laugh

It All Started With A Handful Of Dimes

*B*ehind every good song, there is usually a story.

I like to think that the song, *"Mr. Songman",* as recorded by *"Elvis Presley,"* is a good song. I wrote it and here's *"My Story."*

In March of 1973, I was sitting alone in a booth at a little *"greasy spoon"* here in Nashville, Tennessee. On the wall, at the end of my table, was an old fashioned, table jukebox and every booth had one. I was feeding mine from the handful of dimes I had laying on the table top.

I had worked a late night session as the bass player on a country session at R.C.A. Studio B and had retreated to my favorite *"after midnight"* palace of solitude on the lower end of Broadway where all the musical *"souls of the night"* hung out.

The tiny restaurant was well known to all of the Nashville session musicians and was called *"Linebaugh's."*

At the time, I was going through a marital breakdown and rather than going home to an *"empty house"* at the close of my session, I chose to sponsor a lengthy *"pity party"* and I had only invited *"myself."*

When one needs emotional comfort, I can assure you that a jukebox is not the optimal source. Especially not the ones at Linebaugh's. Every *"cry in your beer"* song of the early 70's could be found among the selections that were waiting for your dime.

I was scheduled to go back to Memphis in two days to rejoin my friend Elvis and that could have contributed to the fact that I had repeatedly been playing his versions of *"Separate Ways"* and *"You Were Always On My Mind."*

It was getting extremely late and I was down to only a few more dimes. I retrieved one from the table and due to the absence of anyone else to talk to, I said to the jukebox, *"Here's another dime for ya Mister Songman"* and once again started listening to *"Separate Ways."*

The song began to play and my thoughts drifted to Elvis and some of the trauma, that I personally knew, he was experiencing from his recent filing for a divorce. Not being able to see his face, Elvis didn't seem as lonely coming from the safety of the jukebox.

No one was paying any attention to me and I struck up a conversation with the unseen Elvis as he continued to sing away my night.

As Elvis sang his songs, the songwriter in me began birthing *"lyric lines"* that I felt might be useful later on, during one of my song writing sessions. I didn't want to lose them so I thought it might be a good idea to write them down.

I had a manila folder full of papers from my earlier session and I took a page out, turned it over and asked the little waitress if I could borrow her pen. The lines started coming more rapidly than those of any other song I have ever written and with the exception of only a few edits, this is what I left Linebaugh's with that lonely morning:

MR. SONGMAN

Here's another dime for you, Mr. Songman
Sing the loneliness of broken dreams away, if you can
Guess, it's only me and you, Mr. Songman
Take away the night, sing away my hurt, Mr. Songman

In your iv'ry covered palace, safe behind your walls of glass
You keep starin' back at me like a mem'ry from the past
Won't you sing me away to a summer night
let me hold her in my arms again
I know mem'ries not relivin' but at least it's not the end

Guess, it's only me and you, Mr. Songman
Take away the night, sing away my hurt, Mr. Songman

Two days later I rejoined Elvis in Memphis. Shortly after my return to Graceland, I was playing the piano in Elvis' piano room and I set the lyrics to music. I titled the tune, *"Mr. Songman."* That same week, my group, *"Voice"* learned the song and we intended to record it at some point and it very quickly became a standard for our *"Elvis' living room concerts."* Among all the songs that Elvis would ask us to sing to him every night, *"Mr. Songman,"* was near the top of the list.

In September of 1973, Elvis and all *"The King's Men"* were relaxing for a few days at his Palm Springs, California home and during the morning of September 8, *"Colonel Tom Park,"* Elvis' manager, called Elvis and reminded him, that due to contractual agreements with RCA Records, they had only a few more days to have a project ready for release and further instructed Elvis to return to Los Angeles, *"git into the studio and git 'a record finished."*

Although not privy to both ends of the conversation, I did hear Elvis' response. I heard him say into the phone, *"Tell 'em, if they want my voice, they gonna have to come down here and git it."*

With God, *"all things"* are possible! With Colonel Parker, *"most things"* were possible!

For that reason, it should have been no surprise to anyone, when early the next morning, on September 9, a huge tractor-trailer truck pulled

up in front of Elvis' front door. Three men promptly jumped out of the truck and began to unload equipment. Within a short time, they had transformed Elvis' living room into a state of the art recording studio and Elvis was soon to begin the creation of songs for his album release, *"Promised Land."*

On Elvis' discography profile, the credits for the project bear the names of recording studios and recording dates that reflect only the place and time that the overdubs were finally completed and not the actual dates of conception. I know! *"I was there!"*

Having had no prior knowledge of the upcoming event, Elvis had not chosen a single song nor contracted a solitary musician but *"Charlie Hodge,"* Elvis' closest friend, had been given this responsibility by the Colonel, the day before. Charlie had tried to schedule all of the *"T.C.B."* band members and get them to Palm Springs on a moment's notice but had been unsuccessful in doing so because most of them had prior commitments to other various artists. He was only able to schedule *"James Burton,"* Elvis' long-time, lead guitar player. Charlie had arranged for James to fly into Palm Springs the night before and he was *"in house"* shortly after the *"living room studio"* had finally been prepared.

We were all in the living room when Elvis came into the room. He reached over and grabbed a microphone, walked over to a big wooden coffee table, stood up on the table said in a *"preacher type"* voice, *"Dearly beloved, we are gathered here today in the presence of these witnesses to make a record and I have one simple question to ask y'all, 'What'n the heck we gonna' record'?"* As we did a lot of times, in response to his unique style of entertaining us guys, we had a big belly laugh.

Then with a more serious tone he asked, *"Really, what we gonna' sing?"* As though the *"we"* of the question truly mattered.

James Burton began playing some ole fashioned *"rock-abilly"* licks on the guitar to which Elvis began to respond with those unique rhythmic sounds that only he was capable of rendering. Charlie Hodge joined in by playing drums on a cardboard box and eventually Elvis broke into a version of *"Promised Land."*

When *"Promised Land"* got boring, Elvis repeated a statement that my Uncle *"J.D. Sumner"* had used on many occasions when it was about time to shut down an Elvis *"living room sing-a long." "Well, if all minds and hearts are clear let's stand and be dismissed."* Then Elvis ended the statement with, *"I'm out 'a songs!"*

Then with *"me"* playing the electric piano, *"Charlie Hodge"* playing drums on his cardboard box, *"James Burton"* rockin' out on his guitar and *"Tim Baty"* the baritone singer in my group Voice, on the bass guitar, we all enjoyed a jam session for a bit while Elvis got with *"Sonny West"* and *"Red West"* his bodyguards, trying to figure out what in the world Elvis was going to put on tape.

Very unexpectedly, Elvis hollered over to me and said, *"Hey, Donnie! Write down the words to 'Mr. Songman'!"* I responded by doing what I always did when I was asked to do something by Elvis, *"I did it!"* and right there in Elvis' living room: with no producer, with no song list prepared, with no back ground vocalist and only a band of amateurs, *"Promised Land"* and my song, *"Mr. Songman,"* began a list of tunes that would soon be found on *"one more"* of Elvis' many great albums.

Many hours later, fifteen songs were *"in the can"* and were being swiftly delivered to *"Felton Jarvis,"* Elvis' R.C.A. Producer. Among those fifteen songs were *"two of mine."* Felton later went into the various studios, on the dates listed in Elvis' discography profile and overdubbed *"The T.C.B Band," "The Sweet Inspirations," "The Stamps Quartet,"* along with my group, *"Voice."*

If I had known, when I was writing lyrics at Linebaugh's, that I would soon be enjoying the luxury of having *"Elvis sing my song"* I probably would have tried to write a few more!

64

Thanks Elvis!
For
The "Memory"
and
The "Sweet Sound Of Your Voice!"

- Donnie Sumner

A Song
is not a song:

Until

"Someone Sings It"

Look For The Good

*I*n every situation of life there is at least *"one"* good element to be found.

For a considerable number of years I have tried to exercise that philosophy when experiencing an unpleasant period. Sometimes the good is difficult to find but it will eventually come to light if you diligently search for it.

In 1972, my marriage had begun to unravel and as time progressed, my ex-wife and I drifted further and further apart. In spite of the negative emotions during our marital demise, I can now report that at least one good thing came from the experience.

For the preceding eight years I had served as the lead vocalist for *"J. D. Sumner and The Stamps Quartet,"* During the last three years of my tenure with The Stamps, *"our group,"* along with *"Kathy Westmoreland," "The Sweet Inspirations"* and *"Charlie Hodge,"* sang together as the vocal ensemble that backed Elvis on all of his records and stage performances.

Immediately following Elvis' *"Aloha"* concert, I resigned my position with The Stamps and organized my own *"pop"* group, known as *"The Rangers."* For the next few weeks, *"I,"* along with *"Shaun Nielsen"* and *"Time Baty,"* sang backup vocals for the *"country stars"* on Nashville's *"Grand Ole Opry."*

In March of that same year, Elvis hired the three of us to be his *"in house"* gospel group. Each of us had been in the nation's top Gospel Quartets and at Elvis' invitation, we became a part of *"the Elvis family"* and from that time forward, we lived and traveled with him constantly. Elvis considered us great vocalists and as our *"boss,"* he decided to change the name of our group to, *"Voice."* Our designated job description was to *"sing gospel music"* to him every night in the privacy of his own living room.

In addition to the privilege of *"living with"* and *"singing for"* Elvis, he also made us a part of his background ensemble and gave us the additional thrill of having the opportunity to open up all of his shows.

In late May of 1973, Elvis had just concluded a series of performances in Lake Tahoe, Nevada and we had returned to Memphis for a few days of rest before his next tour which was to begin in a few days.

It was way after midnight one evening during that particular *"down period,"* and everyone at the *"Graceland Mansion"* had gone to bed. I remained awake and had gone into the downstairs *"piano room"* in hopes of writing a new song. I was engrossed in what I was doing and had failed to hear Elvis come up behind me and although I was startled when I saw him, it was, as *"always,"* a thrill to be joined by *"Elvis!"*

He just wanted to *"talk to somebody"* and in-as-much as I was the only one awake, I had been chosen to be that person.

We were both experiencing the erosion of our marriages and for the next hour or so, we just sat there talking, like two high school guys discussing our breakups with our respective girlfriends. To anyone who doubts Elvis' love for Priscilla, I truly wish you could have experienced the emotion in his voice when once, during our conversation, he said, *"God! I miss that woman!"*

Eventually, Elvis returned to his *"upstairs hide-away"* and I continued on with my song writing. As I worked, I couldn't get my mind off of what we both had told each other and the loneliness that we were both experiencing. The statement that Elvis had made, *"God! I miss that woman,"* along with others that he had made during our talk, kept reoccurring and before anyone else awakened, I pretty much had penned our entire conversation into a set of lyrics that read:

I MISS YOU

Still, I recall all the good times together
The love we shared, the fun and the laughter
How I wish you could feel what my heart says tonight, dear
How I miss you and I wish you were here

Dreams that I had, they lay broken in sorrow
The plans I made, my hopes for tomorrow
If I could, I would tell you I'm lonesome tonight, dear
Lord! I miss you and I wish you were here

All through the night, I will see mem'ries passing
The way you looked, the sound of you laughing
How I long for the touch of your hand holding my, dear
God! I miss you and I wish you were here

With those lyrics still in my mind, I went to Graceland's downstairs bedroom, adjacent to the music lounge and went to sleep.

I eventually put music to my lyrics. Voice learned the song and we would often sing it to Elvis at night but never once, during our *"living room"* renditions of my song, did I ever consider the possibility that it would soon come to life in an *"Elvis"* recording. But *"it did!"*

September of that year, found all the *"Elvis guys"* in Palm Springs, California. It was always a thrill to visit Elvis' home in Palm Springs and I experienced a number of *"firsts"* inside its walls. It was in Palm Springs that I took my first lesson in the martial arts. It was there that I shared my first session of meditation with Elvis and it was in his Palm Springs living room, on September 9, 1973, that I first heard Elvis sing one of my songs.

Early during the morning that day, at the unexpected command of *"Colonel Tom Parker,"* Elvis' manager, R.C.A. Records drove into Palm Springs with a mobile studio and upon their arrival, they set up their entire operation in *"Elvis' living room."* No one in Elvis' entourage had been notified of the session until the previous day: Therefore, there was very little time to compile a song list and hire studio musicians for the event. The only member of the *"T.C.B."* band that was available was *"James Burton"* and he had flown into Palm Springs the night before on Elvis' private jet.

Soon after R.C.A. had finished their setup, everything was ready except for a list of songs that Elvis wanted to record. Elvis got with *"Sonny West"* and *"Red West,"* his bodyguards in an effort to figure out, in Elvis' words, *"What'n the heck am I gonna sing!"*

The next thing I knew, Elvis was asking me to write down the lyrics to some of the original songs that Voice had been singing for him during our nightly presentations.

The list included, *"Help Me"* by Larry Gatlin; *"Love Song Of The Year"* by Chris Christian; *"I Never Stopped Thinking About You"* by Tim Baty" and two of my songs, *"Mr. Songman"* and the song that I had written at Graceland, *"I Miss You."*

Then, with only *"James Burton,"* of the T.C.B. Band, on his Fender guitar; *"Tim Baty,"* of Voice, on the bass guitar; *"Charlie Hodge,"* Elvis' closest friend, using a cardboard box as a snare drum and *"me"* on a Fender Rhodes electric piano, as *"his band:"* Elvis recorded the entire list of lyrics he had

asked me to write down.

The night ended with all five of those songs, plus ten more, on their  way to various studios for *"Felton Jarvis,"* Elvis' producer to complete and mix down.

During October of 1973, R.C.A. released a brand new project by *"Elvis Presley"* under the title *"Raised On Rock."* Among the songs listed on the back cover was my song, *"I Miss You!"*

As I look back on it now, I could have never imagined that a song would be birthed by a conversation that I once had with *"my friend, Elvis,"* one lonely night at Graceland: but amid all of the unpleasantness of my past marital failure, it seems that my philosophy, *"Look For The Good!"* really does have merit. It was during one of my life's *"low points"* that I was gifted with the reward of having *"Elvis record two of my songs!"*

And that, boys and girls, is *"Good!"*

- Donnie Sumner

Without The Valleys: There Could Be No Mountaintops!

Don't Mention It Around Elvis

"If it ain't broke, don't fix it!"

At least that's *"my"* philosophy and if my looks seems to be less than perfect, please don't bring me discomfort in order to change 'em.

My friend Elvis was of an opposite opinion. If there was an imperfection in your appearance and money could fix it, you better not mention it in his presence or you might be setting yourself up for a big surprise.

I have a large scar across the bridge of my nose, two oddly shaped and very large ears, along with a few other minor flaws and I am extremely grateful that all of the above went *"unnoticed"* by Elvis during the times we spent together.

Let me tell you why!

In September of 1973, Elvis took us all to Palm Springs, California for a few days of rest. The second night we were there, all the guys were sitting with Elvis in the living room kidding each other about who was the *"best looking"* and over a period of a few minutes each person had made a humorous comment about someone else in the group.

Because we were the newest men in the group, *"Shaun Nielsen, Tim Baty and myself"* felt a little uneasy about kidding the *"long-standing"* members of the gang and therefore we had made no jesting overtures at this point.

Elvis, keenly aware, as he always was, abruptly realized that neither Shaun, Tim nor myself, had joined in with a poking comment and with an unexpected, big laugh he said, *"I guess the only ones perfect in here is me and Voice!"*

Shaun giggled and replied, *"I keep all mine covered up."* Elvis asked, *"What 'cha' coverin' up man? Ya look OK to me."* Shaun said back to him, *"Well, my hair's a little thin on the top and I have to comb it up from the sides to cover it up."*

Then pointing to his teeth, Shaun went on to say, *"I've always had this tiny space here between my teeth, so I just don't smile too big and not too many people notice it."*

After a little more conversation among ourselves, Elvis decided he wanted to sing some *"gospel"* songs and after a lengthy night of singing, everybody went to bed.

The next morning, Elvis called Voice into the living room and as we came into the room Elvis said, *"Hey guys, I want 'cha to meet my friend, Dr. Shapiro."*

After the introductions were made and hands were shaken, Elvis pointed to a recliner adjacent to the couch and said to Shaun, *"Go over there and sit down. Dr. Shapiro's gonna' fix that space between ya teeth!"*

Shaun moved over to the chair, sat down and prepared himself as though he was about to watch a movie.

Dr. Shapiro got up, went over to the side of the living room and brought back with him an electric motor mounted on a piece of plywood and placed it on the coffee table. To that apparatus, he then attached an *"old fashioned,"* *"belt driven,"* flexible arm that held a dental drill.

In just a few minutes Shaun got up from the couch smiling and there for all the world to see were *"two beautiful caps,"* compliments of Elvis.

The end? *"Not on your life!"*

After Dr. Shapiro left, we all went into the dining room to eat. Just as we were finishing our lunch, the doorbell rang.

"Red West," Elvis' bodyguard, went to the door, opened it and invited the person standing there to, *"Come on in!"* Responding to his welcome from Red, a short gentleman of oriental descent came through the door. I can neither pronounce nor spell his name but I can definitely tell you *"what"* he was and *"why"* he had come.

Elvis got up, shook the man's hand and shouted back toward us, *"Hey, Shaun! Come here! I got 'a surprise for ya. The Doc's here to give ya a hair transplant."*

I was expecting Shaun to lose his newly acquired caps but instead, he casually followed Elvis into the bedroom where the Doctor instructed him to lie down on the bed.

Elvis and the Doctor took a bed sheet, cut out a small circle in it and draped it over Shaun's body with Shaun's head centered inside the hole. Then, with all of us standing around the walls of the bedroom watching, the Doctor proceeded to remove one hundred small plugs of hair from the backside of Shaun's head and insert them into one hundred small holes he had previously made in the top of his scalp.

Having successfully completed the procedure, the Doctor then wrapped Shaun's entire head in a huge thick blanket of gauze. When Shaun finally stood up, he looked like Hollywood's *"Invisible Man."*

After that experience, if I ever looked in the mirror and saw something I didn't like, I immediately said to myself:

"Don't mention it around Elvis!"

- Donnie Sumner

It takes both
Rain and Sunshine
To Make A Rainbow

A Little Flat There "Buddy"

*N*o singer allows a project to be released with *"off-pitch"* vocal notes.

No one except *"Elvis,"* that is!

The *"only"* such work I know of that has ever been released was approved by Elvis and was done so for a personal and very special reason.

In September of 1973, Elvis' home in Palm Springs, California was temporarily transformed into a multi-purpose facility. It became both a *"medical clinic"* and *"a recording studio."*

On the eighth of that month, Elvis made *"Shaun Nielsen,"* the tenor singer in my group, *"Voice,"* the recipient of *"two dental crowns"* and a *"one hundred plug hair transplant."* Elvis' living room was used as

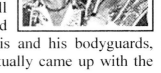

the dental lab for Shaun's crowns and Elvis' bedroom was turned into a surgical unit for his hair transplant procedure.

The next day, on the morning of September 9, R.C.A. Records invaded Elvis' home and set up a state of the art, mobile recording studio in his living room. During the coarse of the next few hours, *"Elvis, Charlie Hodge, James Burton"* and my group *"Voice,"* successfully recorded the rough tracks for songs that would eventually be released as Elvis' *"Promised Land"* and *"Raised On Rock"* projects.

We had worked all day and it was becoming quite late. Everyone was rather tired but we still needed one more song to fill out the predefined number of cuts. After some debate between Elvis and his bodyguards, *"Red West and Sonny West,"* together, they eventually came up with the song *"Are You Sincere."*

After the song had been suggested, our little four piece band began the intro and Elvis ran through it a couple of times. During the rehearsal run- throughs, Elvis came up with the idea that he wanted *"Shaun Nielsen,"* the tenor of *"Voice,"* to do a short obbligato repeat line of the words, *"Are You Sincere"* at the end of the song, much like *"Kathy Westmoreland"* would have done, had she been present. Elvis thought Shaun possessed one of the nicest lyric tenor voices he had ever heard and loved for Shaun to sing songs for him that allowed Shaun to exploit the unique quality of his soft tenor sounds. Everyone was working at full capacity: *"all"* except *"Shaun."*

Having just experienced two lengthy and painful medical procedures the day before, Shaun was enduring considerable pain and discomfort. He was endeavoring to manage the pain by taking a few painkillers. Though still able to function, Shaun was in no way capable of maximum performance.

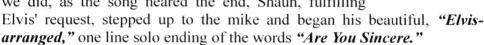

After a few rehearsal attempts, we finally got around to the actual recording process. On the first cut we did, as the song neared the end, Shaun, fulfilling Elvis' request, stepped up to the mike and began his beautiful, *"Elvis-arranged,"* one line solo ending of the words *"Are You Sincere."*

To no ones surprise, *"Are you sin-"* came out with exquisite clarity

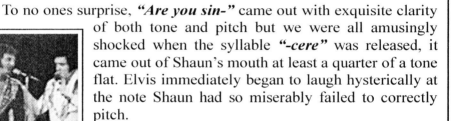

of both tone and pitch but we were all amusingly shocked when the syllable *"-cere"* was released, it came out of Shaun's mouth at least a quarter of a tone flat. Elvis immediately began to laugh hysterically at the note Shaun had so miserably failed to correctly pitch.

After the rush of laughter from all of us had subsided, Shaun with his gauze covered head and his pain-killer numbed body approached Elvis and said, *"I gotta' overdub that ending, boss! I really blew it!"*

Elvis laughed and surprised everyone when he said to Shaun, *"That's the first time I ever heard 'you' miss a pitch and I want the whole world to hear it just to prove to 'em you can't sing as good as me!"*

When *"Felton Jarvis,"* Elvis' R.C.A. producer, finally mixed and edited the song, he erased Elvis' laughing seizure on the end of *"Are You Sincere,"* but Shaun's note remains flat to this day, *"thanks to Elvis."*

If Heaven's eternity has a CD player, I suppose, that on occasion, Elvis still listens to *"Are You Sincere"* and has a big laugh.

I know for sure that, here on earth, I do!

- Donnie Sumner

Mistakes are like Footprints
If you go anywhere ... You'll Make At Least One

The Devil Came To Hollywood

I love angels but I hate demons!

It's no wonder that I have a fearful respect for the occult. My Dad was a *"hell fire and brimstone"* Pentecostal preacher and I was exposed to many sermons concerning *"demonic powers."*

Although I've heard numerous accounts of demonic attacks, I have no personal knowledge of such an event. I have never been confronted with a demon spirit but there was once a night that *"I thought I was!"*

In December of 1973, Elvis complet-ed several nights of recording at Stax studio in Memphis. Christ-mas was coming on and he wanted to have a *"private Christmas celebration"* at *"Grace-land,"* so, he flew us all to *"Hollywood"* for a Christmas party with *"all of us."* Boys and girls, I can assure you that Elvis' Monovale Drive home in Hollywood was definitely *"a great place to celebrate Christmas!"*

As part of our activities, Elvis rented the screening room of M.G.M. studios for our private viewing of a movie that had just been released. I should have known that I was gonna have some serious moments of anxiety when I heard the name of the move: *"The Exorcist!"*

If per chance you have never seen the movie, it tells the story of a young girl that had become *"demon possessed."* The special effects in the movie were especially realistic and the beauty of the leading actress, Linda Blair, became more and more hideous as the movie progressed. Before the movie ended she was flying around the room, bouncing off walls, speaking in a man's voice and had the appearance of a *"zombie!"* To say that it was *"a frightening presentation"* would be an understatement.

I associate a lot of things with Christmas but among my personal choices, watching *"The Exorcist"* would probably not have been one of them. I have to confess; That film really had me in a *"dither"* by the time it concluded and to this day, if and when I see advertisements for a similar presentation advertised on my television screen, my thumb becomes very active as it begins searching for another channel.

"I love angels but I hate demons!"

When the film was over, the group jumped back into the three limousines that had brought us to the M.G.M. lot and we headed back to Elvis' Belair home.

Once we had arrived, Elvis went into his bedroom for a *"clothes change"* and the rest of us headed straight for the den. As I usually did, I started a big *"multi-color"* fire in the den's large fireplace so that it would be roaring by the time Elvis decided to join us.

It didn't seem like Elvis was gonna come out of his room for a while, so, *"Ricky Stanley,"* Elvis' step brother, and I decided we would go into Elvis' *"big T.V. and game room"* to watch television by ourselves. Now friend, when I say *"big,"* I definitely mean *"big!"* In the middle of the room was a plush leather, *"U-shaped couch"* that could seat twenty-one people very comfortably.

With no shortage of space, Ricky and I lay back, full length, on opposite sides of the couch and started watching the *"Cal Worthington Movie Channel."* Cal was one of the nation's largest auto dealers with numerous car lots in the Los Angeles area. He owned and operated his own television station and his personal commercials were the only ones it aired. Each commercial was a funny little skit all its own.  One of my favorites showed him riding on the back of *"Shamu The Whale."* Several of *"Johnny Carson's"* skits came from watching the Cal Worthington commercials. Cal's station only aired movies and regardless of the time, day or night, you could always depend on *"Ol' Cal"* being on line with a movie and his funny commercials.

At this point, I can't remember the name of the movie that Ricky and I were watching but I can definitely remember what happened during its presentation.

Apparently, Elvis had joined the other guys in the den and had noticed that Ricky and I were missing. The only thing that Elvis ever needed to pull a prank was *"an opportunity"* and I guess it seemed to him that one had just dropped from the sky.

Where it came from I will never know but somewhere in the house, Elvis had found the most hideous looking *"monster face mask"* I have ever seen.

Unbeknownst to Ricky and myself, Elvis had donned the mask and had quietly sneaked into the T.V. and game room.

As I lay there enjoying a *"non-demon"* movie. *"I was suddenly attacked by one!"*

Elvis had slithered around to the end of the couch on my side and he suddenly stuck his *"mask-covered"* head up above the end, grabbed my feet and let out a very large and audible, *"Arrrrgh!"*

After I had gained a little composure, I turned around and there in the doorway stood *"Sonny West, Red West, Charlie Hodge and Jerry Schilling,"* laughing their crazy heads off.

I have never *"wet my pants"* from fright but I almost did, *"twice in one night."* Once when Linda Blair almost jumped into my lap while I was watching *"The Exorcist"* and shortly thereafter when *"the demon"* grabbed my feet in Elvis' T.V. and game room.

I love Angels
BUT I HATE DEMONS!

- Donnie Sumner

Penicillan Can't Cure
A Good Scare!
But
A Good Laugh Will!

Be Careful Where You Park

*W*hen Elvis says, *"vacation"* … He means, *"VACATION!"*

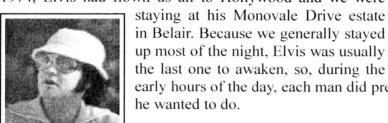

One morning, at the beginning of the Summer in 1974, Elvis had flown us all to Hollywood and we were staying at his Monovale Drive estate in Belair. Because we generally stayed up most of the night, Elvis was usually the last one to awaken, so, during the early hours of the day, each man did pretty much what he wanted to do.

On one particular morning during our time there, I was sitting alone in Elvis' den watching television. I was laid back in a really plush leather recliner, savoring the pleasure of being in Elvis' house, when *"the boss"* walked into the room and quietly sat down on the long coach that stretched across the room.

We started a general conversation and soon the context of our thoughts turned toward the joys of the season that was upon us.

School had just let out in Nashville and for some reason, I brought up the subject of my son and daughter in regard to what I thought they might be doing for the next three months. During the conversation, Elvis asked me if I had planned a vacation with them. I answered, *"Well boss, when it comes to home time, I never make any plans. If their Mother wants to plan one, I guess it will be just the three of 'em, 'cause I'm gonna be here with you."*

When Elvis asked me how long since I had seen my children, I responded with the answer. Elvis surprised me when he said, *"Man you need to go home for a few days or you're 'kids' are gonna start callin' ya 'Mr. Daddy'."*

As the minutes passed, word must have gotten around the house that *"Elvis was up"* because, one by one, all the guys soon found themselves in the den with Elvis and I. As usual, when all the bunch got into one room, we began to laugh and have a good time enjoying each other's friendship.

Under normal circumstances, my earlier conversation with Elvis would have passed with no consequence but on this occasion, that was not to be the case.

Late that night, Elvis called me aside, into the privacy of his living room, and told me that he wanted me to take ten days and *"go have a vacation with your family."* Furthermore, he said, *"It's on me!"* He then handed me a credit card that *"Joe Espisito,"* his personal road manager, usually carried for incidentals and said, *"Have a ball!"*

I asked him, *"When do want me to start?"* Elvis responded with *"Tomorrow morning and I've already made arrangement for your travel!"*

Early the next morning, I was in Elvis' kitchen area eating a big breakfast that his housekeeper had prepared for me. I suspected that I was gonna need some serious food before I boarded, what I thought was to be *"the plane."*

To the surprise of both the sweet little housekeeper and myself, Elvis came walking into the kitchen, fully dressed in his *"unique style"* everyday wardrobe. To see Elvis handsomely dressed was not unusual but to see him *"all decked out"* that early in the morning certainly was.

Elvis walked over to me and said, *"Come outside. I got somethin' I wanna show ya."* We walked out of the kitchen, thru the living room and out thru the front door and there, parked in his driveway, was a luxurious 1974, thirty-two foot, green and white Executive motor coach. *(The night before, Elvis had Joe Espisito to make all the arrangements and have the coach delivered by daylight.)*

Elvis reached into one of his pockets and pulled out a notarized title to the vehicle. He reached into another pocket and when his hand came out, it was holding a set of keys suspended from a lightning bolt style keychain. He reached his hand out, handed me both articles and then with a giggling smile said, *"It's yours, so keep 'er between the white lines."*

Together, we walked toward the bus. When we got to the coach, Elvis opened the door, stepped inside and I did the same. To my amazement, behind the steering wheel of the vehicle sat a young man I had never met. Elvis said, *"Donnie, this is Jim Thompson, he's gonna be ya new bodyguard. He's gonna drive ya to Nashville, fly back and be here waitin' when ya get back."*

Who would have ever imagined that, someday, *"Ol' Donnie"* would need a *"personal bodyguard?"* The truth is, *"I didn't!"*

Elvis only *"thought"* I needed one! I should have reminded him that: If anybody ever got after me, with legs as long as mine are, I could outrun them.

Within the hour, after a lot of *"Thank You's!"* to Elvis, Ol' Donnie was heading eastward, watching videos in his brand new chariot. Once we arrived in Nashville, I took Jim to the airport and then drove myself home. It was about thirty minutes from the airport to my house and during the entire ride I kept trying to figure out where I was gonna take my kids.

My wife and I were not enjoying a particularly wonderful relationship during that time period and I had not called home in several days. When I showed up at the door to our home, she met me with, *"What'n the world are you doin' home. I thought you were in California."* I said back to her, *"I was until day before yesterday, but Elvis told me to come home and take a vacation with y'all. So, 'Here I Is'!"* When she asked me where the bus came from, I smiled and said, *"It's mine! Elvis gave it to me!"*

After packin' everything we were gonna need, we hit the road. We had *"no plans"* and we were headed *"no place special"* but we eventually, found ourselves in Brunswick, Georgia and I decided I wanted to stay on the beach at Jekyll Island. Most folks would have gotten a motel but not me: I drove the bus right out onto the beach and parked it with the side window facing the water.

With the sound of the waves coming thru the window, what a night that was; But with all of my ingenuity, I had failed to consider the ocean tide changes. Unbeknownst to me, during the night, the tide had come in and the next morning, as I started to step out onto the sandy beach, I discovered that we were sitting in about ten to twelve inches of water.

Have you ever eaten breakfast in *"a bus sitting in the ocean?"* *"I have!"* The good news is:

Just like a hairline, the ocean edge will eventually recede.

I live by the philosophy, *"Look For The Good"* and here's *"The Good News"* in my recollection? I have done something that Elvis never dreamed of or much-less did.

"I Drove A Bus Into The Atlantic Ocean!"

"Thanks Elvis"
for a
"Tremendous Gift"
and a
"Great Memory"

- Donnie Sumner

When you Live with
ELVIS

EVERY DAY
and
EVERY WHERE
IS A VACATION!

The Hairless Drummer

I don't know if you've ever seen an Indian *"head scalping"* but I have. At least that's the way it appeared at the time.

I don't recall the exact date but it was sometime toward the middle of 1975 during one of Elvis' Las Vegas Hilton engagements.

The Hilton always featured Elvis in the main showroom and scheduled other big name artists to play the lounge during his tenure there. Either, *"B.B. King, Red Foxx, Bill Medley of the Righteous Brothers or Chubby Checker"* were always engaged by the Hilton to headline as second billing with the Elvis Show. Elvis played Vegas a lot and because of his frequent Hilton schedules and the regularity of the co-artist's engagements, he had become very good friends with all of them.

When in Vegas, it was our regular routine to meet in Elvis' suite at the Hilton after his second show each night. Because they had become Elvis' friends, he had also given an open invitation to the lounge stars to be his late night guest in the suite, any time they so desired.

Several of the other Vegas hotels had regularly scheduled stars that they always contracted to coincide with the time frame of Elvis' Hilton schedule. Over the years, Elvis developed a close friendship with several

of these celebrities and some of them were present practically every night. *"Tom Jones, Bobby Gentry, Jack Lord and Marty Allen"* were those most often present.

There was always a large number of guests in Elvis' suite at the close of his night's work.

During Elvis' shows there were always several stuffed animals and other small items that were thrown onto the stage and it was the duty of *"Charlie Hodge,"* Elvis' close friend and stage companion, to pick them all up and bring them to the suite each night. When Charlie got to the suite each night, he would take all the little trinkets that he had picked up and place them on the bar and other visible places in the room. It was common knowledge that if a guest wanted one of these little items as a souvenir of their visit with Elvis, they were at liberty to take one home with them. And right there, boys and girls, is where the story begins.

One this particular summer night, Elvis had successfully concluded his midnight show and we were enjoying our evening as his guest in the luxury of his suite. In attendance that night was *"Chubby Checker."* Chubby had frequently been Elvis' guest but he had always come alone. This night, his lead guitar player and his drummer were with him and I draw particular attention to the *"drummer."* I never knew the drummer's name but I definitely remember his *"persona."*

Chubby's drummer was dressed quite flamboyantly when he entered the suite. He was donned in a pink, waist length, coat jacket completely covered with sequins; a pair of red leather pants; a frilly, lime green shirt and lime green, four inch heeled boots also covered with sequins. His accessories included a long strapped, sequined, shoulder purse that hung to just below his waist. In addition to his unusual ensemble, he also sported very long and straight hair that came to well below his shoulders.

I was fascinated by the drummer's apparel but I wasn't alone. His attire was well noticed by everyone in the room. He drew attention to himself, regardless of where he might find himself or to whom he might be talking at any given moment and all throughout the evening he was extremely visible.

"Red West and Sonny West" were both very kind hearted and gentle men but they were both like *"Mama Bears"* protecting a set of cubs when it came to Elvis and his *"close friend guests."*

All evening long, Red and Sonny had their hands full endeavoring to keep the *"little drummer boy"* from having direct contact with Elvis because trying to *"out-glitz"* Elvis is something one should not try if they are a guest in his home.

It had become quite late and Chubby, his guitar play and several of the other guests had exited the room. Upon their leaving, several of them had chosen a little item from the stage treasures and had claimed it as their own. It was *"O.K."* and Chubby's drummer had observed it all.

Among the items, out in the open, was a small and very cute music box that had been given to *"Linda Thompson,"* Elvis' lady companion. She had been playing it earlier and had mistakenly left it on the bar counter near the other small items. It was still open and had completely run down.

Chubby's drummer finally decided that it was time to call it a night and was preparing to leave the suite. I was behind the bar cleaning up a little when he came over to the bar, picked up Linda's little music box and put it inside his purse.

That was his first mistake!

Red West, vigilant as always, saw the drummer put the music box in his purse. Red knew that the music box was not one of the items available to the guests and he approached the drummer with Sonny West right behind him. When Red got to the little gentleman, he explained to him that the music box was Linda Thompson's personal property and could not be taken from the suite.

Apparently, the drummer was offended because he began to argue with Red as to the fact that it was among the items that had been offered to the guests. Red tried to explain to him that Linda had left it there by mistake and that it was definitely not his for the taken. The little guy became more and more verbal and was drawing attention to the situation.

That was his second mistake!

It finally reached the point where Red and Sonny began to escort him toward the door of the suite. By the time they got to the door, the drummer was really getting loud and *"everyone"* in the room had become

 aware of what was happening. With Red on one side and Sonny on the other, the three of them approached the door. Red opened the door with one hand and began to lead the guy into the suite's foyer. Chubby's drummer abruptly turned around and with both hands shoved Red backwards into the door frame.

That was his third mistake!

Both Red and Sonny were highly trained in the martial arts and were experts in the art of self defense.

When the drummer pushed Red, he instinctively went into a defense mode. It was like a ballet. Red came up with his left arm drove the drummer's left arm and hand downward. At the same instant, he extended his right arm straight forward and with a closed fist hit the startled fellow right in the middle of his chest. The guy was struck with so much force that he fell backward and was wound up sprawled out on the floor of the foyer.

Red immediately jumped on top of him with his knees resting on each side of the man's chest. I guess Red was planning to really *"knock his block off"* because he drew back his right fist and at the same time reached out with his left hand, grabbed the drummer's hair and attempted to pull his head forward so that he could get a better angle on the guy's chin.

To everyone's amazement, when Red pulled at the fellow's hair, it came completely of the boy's head. I wish you could have seen it. There was Red sitting astride a man's chest with both hands in the air. One hand was closed into a fist and the other was holding a very long-haired *"wig!"*

Elvis had reached the doorway by this time and when he saw Red kneeling there, holding the drummer's wig, he hollered out, *"My God Red! You've scalped him!"* Red dropped the wig, rolled off the guy, sat down on the floor and with everyone joining in; started laughing really hard.

 Still laughing, Red, Sonny and Elvis came back into the suite and closed the door. Before they came back in, Elvis had picked up the wig and had it in his hand when he re-entered. He held it up like a trophy and *"Charlie Hodge"* asked him what he was gonna do with it. Elvis said, *"This poor pilgrim was a good man and we're gonna have a proper burial!"* He then laid the wig on the bar counter and began going the motions of a priest giving *"last rites."*

It goes without saying that *"Elvis' liturgical efforts"* were just as funny as the scalping and between the two events, we all enjoyed an extremely large amount of hearty laugher.

As we had done on other occasions, between shows the following night, Elvis' step-brother, *"Ricky Stanley"* and I went into the Hilton lounge to see the Chubby Checker show. The show was presented just as we had seen it before except it appeared that Chubby had a new drummer. His face looked like the previous drummer and he wore similar clothes but *"there wasn't a hair on his head."*

He had been "scalped" by Red West and: Elvis had "embalmed" the scalp!

- Donnie Sumner

There's a real
Upside to Baldnesss:
Your Hair Is Never Messed Up

The New Sheriff's In Town

*"**S**top! Police,"*

To the fleeing perpetrator, I guess it only appeared to be Elvis with his head sticking up thru the roof of a Mercedes limousine but it *"really was the police."* By the way, *"in Hollywood nothing is out of the ordinary!"* So, *"Why stop?"*

Let me tell ya the story!

During the summer of 1974, Elvis had once again taken us all to rest for while in the luxury of his Hollywood home. I can't recall the exact day during that visit, but I do remember the incident very well.

Elvis' Monovale Drive home, in Hollywood, was a very large and meticulously manicured estate, surrounded by a stone fence. Included in the amenities was a large swimming pool with a fully equipped, two bedroom apartment. *"Ricky Stanley,"* Elvis' stepbrother and I always chose to sleep in the pool house when we visited Elvis' Bel Air home.

On this particular morning, Ricky and I were both slumbering in the pool apartment after a long night of singing in the living room with Elvis and I can assure you that when one is *"sacked out"* and enjoying a good sleep, their least anticipated event is *"gittin' up!"*

I guess *"Charlie Hodge,"* Elvis' right hand man, didn't understand that because early that morning, Charlie called us on the house intercom system and said, *"Elvis wants y'all up here ASAP!"* In response to the call from Charlie, We both got out of bed, got dressed and went up to the main house to see what Elvis wanted.

When we got back to the main house, Elvis said to us, *"I want y'all to go shoppin' with me!"* I have been known to do some shopping in my time but *"never with Elvis."* Therefore, I became quite excited at the prospect.

Soon afterward, *"Elvis,"* donned in his *"wow"* attire, along with myself, *"Shaun Nielsen and Tim Baty,"* (the other two guys in my group, Voice) *"Ricky Stanley, Charlie Hodge and Red West,"* all piled into Elvis' limousine and proceeded down the drive and out thru the estate gate to go *"do the town!"*

Shopping with Elvis has a couple of unusual characteristics, especially when done in a men's clothing store!

First of all, Elvis was no expert on sizes, materials or colors and his sales pitch was simple, *"If it shines, it's mine!"*

Secondly, if you pulled anything off the rack and looked at it, Elvis thought you wanted it and the item immediately went into the growing pile of soon-to-be-purchased garments.

After traveling a short distance, we finally arrived at the men's store on Hollywood Boulevard that Elvis had chosen for us to visit.

We all piled out of the limousine, went into the store and within a relatively short period of time we had enough genuine leather jackets, designer jeans and flam-boyant shirts to clothe a small army.

Elvis seemed to be satisfied with our array of loot and he said to Red, *"Pay for it!"* Red pulled out a credit card and paid the cashier. The gentleman serving us handed Red the receipt and with a very *"big"* smile said, *"Thank You!"* Then, with our arms laden with goodies, we all got back into the limousine and started home.

Elvis' limousine had a window between the drivers' seat and the passenger area with two fold up seats positioned against the back of the front seat. These two extra seats would open up and accommodate two extra passengers with them facing the backseat of the automobile. Some of the other amenities included in the limo were personal storage compartments in four places, an intercom sy-stem, and a *"large retractable sun roof."*

When we started finding our seats in the car, Red was the last man in and he got situated in the front seat with Charlie in the middle. Ricky and I settled into the two, rear facing, jump seats. Facing forward on the back seat was Shaun on the left, Tim in the middle and Elvis sitting next to the window on the right. The remaining space was filled with our purchases.

I have to confess, *"one"* of the gentlemen facing the rear was as excited as a kid at Christmas.

As excited as I was, I really didn't know how excited one could really become. Things were about to go from *"shoppin' to shootin'!"*

Driving home, thru the elite area of Bel Air, just a short way from Elvis' home, a small red sports car suddenly came speeding out of a driveway, right in front of Elvis' limousine. Elvis' driver immediately slammed on the brakes and when he did, all of us were thrown into motion. With the exception of the two, rear facing heads that bumped the partition window, no particular damage was done.

None that is, except to Elvis!

When we came to such an abrupt stop, Elvis was thrown forward into the lap of Ricky. Elvis wasn't hurt but it sure did startle him. Elvis pulled himself up, reached over and pushed the button that opened the sun roof and hollered to the driver, *"Catch that car!"*

The roof top scooted back and then, to our surprise, Elvis reached into his personal compartment inside the limo's right hand door and pulled out a gun with a barrel that looked as long as my arm. Holding the gun in his hand, he put his feet on the back seat and stood up thru the sun roof with about half his body sticking thru the opening.

You must remember, we had just been shopping and Elvis was dressed in his full *"Memphis - Beale Street"* regalia. His riding attire in-cluded a *"royal blue, velvet, wide brimmed hat; a short matching royal blue cape; a white bouffant shirt and his very unique sun glasses."*

Elvis' *"hat"* was the first casualty of the moment. When Elvis' head hit open air, *"his hat flew off"* and has never been seen since.

With the sun roof open, the draft from inside the car pulled Elvis' *"cape"* up thru the opening and it began to trail behind him like a flag in a hard blowing wind. If the driver of the fleeing car in front of us had taken the time to look in his rear view mirror, it would probably have appeared to be *"Snoopy"* standing on top of a white car.

But it wasn't, it was just *"my friend and boss, Elvis!"*

It's no secret that Elvis was an honorary member of numerous police forces. In his Graceland home, he had an entire bag full of genuine police badges and several of them were decorated with precious stones.

I don't know if it was the shine of the badges or a childhood fantasy but I do know that Elvis loved to look at them and that he was mighty proud of 'em.

Never-the-less, immediately upon *"gittin' in 'da wind,"* Elvis, as if the little red car had ears, yelled out, *"Stop! Police!"*

I guess it startled Elvis when the car didn't obey his official command, but in response to the car's obvious refusal to stop, Elvis pointed his gun upward and fired a shot into the *"wild blue yonder."*

Elvis' limo did not have nearly as much acceleration as the other car and it was certain that we were not gonna be able to catch up to the fleeing car, so, Elvis lowered himself back into the car, plopped down in his seat and didn't say a word until later that night.

For the remainder of the journey back to Elvis' estate, the limo's interior contained: lots of packages; one embarrassed driver; one long haired step-brother; one concerned bodyguard; four frightened singers and one *"silent superstar!"*

If some warm afternoon, the new tenants of an unknown Monovale Drive estate in Bel Air, California, should be walking around his or her beautiful property and notice a small hole in one of their trees, they just might try to get a little closer to determine what had caused it. If they inves-tigated diligently, he or she just might retrieve a long lost bit of *"metallic memorabilia"* left there by my friend, the late *Elvis Presley.* In all probability the recipient of the treasure would have no idea as to its worth and just simply say to themselves:

"I wonder how in the world this bullet got into my tree!"

I Just Told Ya!

- Donnie Sumner

> Bullets don't bother me:
> I just don't want to be there,
> When They're Flyin'!

The Teacher

I have a very short attention span!

Unless I am really interested in a subject, it usually receives only *"limited concentration"* on my part.

Having tried to avoid educational pursuits for quite a while, during my young years, I was not overly excited when Elvis came into the living room one morning and announced that he was gonna teach my group, *"Voice,"* the art of *"meditation."*

Until this time, my idea of meditation was *"laying back in a leather recliner with my eyes shut."*

That particular morning was during the Summer of 1975 and it found all the members of Voice in the middle of Elvis' living room, *"sitting in a circle"* with Elvis in the middle.

We were all vacationing at Elvis' Palm Springs, California home and Elvis had sent word thru *"Charlie Hodge,"* his faithful companion, that he wanted to see all of *"Voice"* in the living room.

Once we arrived there, Elvis got up, walked over to us and gave each of us a golden, chain necklace with a jade ornament suspended on it. We were told to place it around the top of our heads with the jade ornament resting on our foreheads between our eyebrows. He went on to explain that the ornament that would come to rest on forehead, signified a third, *"all seeing eye,"* and that thru the power of visualization it would allow us to observe our *"inner man."*

Elvis presented us with individual pillows and then invited us to sit down on the floor with him. He began to instruct us on how to assume a Yoga position that is referred to as *"the Lotus position."*

To achieve this pose; you bend your knees and cross your legs with each ankle resting on its opposite thigh. You then extend your arms downward, resting your hands on your knees and with your fingers you form the circle *"O"* by touching your thumb and middle finger together, on each hand. It was only a little uncomfortable at the time but at my present age, *"it 'hurts' just to think about it."*

After each of us had assumed the correct position, we all joined hands, closed our eyes and in a monotone voice, followed Elvis' lead in verbalizing the mantra; *"Christ Life, Christ Peace, Christ Love,"* In unison, we repeated the mantra multiplied times.

After speaking the mantra for a while, Elvis stopped and began explaining to us the word *"Ohm."* In short, *"Ohm"* is the cosmic sound of the universe and that, theoretically, this tone holds the universe together. He then began instructing us on how to use the word *"Ohm,"* along with specific breathing techniques, to acquire a state of total relaxation.

After several minutes of vocal and breathing exercises, Elvis began to explain the value of colors and their ability to create a desired result. For instance, blue for tranquility, green for healing, yellow for happiness etc. We were to practice visualizing friends and family members surrounded by a specific color, suited to the blessing that we wished to transmit into their individual realities.

I sat there repeating the mantra, *"Christ Light, Christ Peace, Christ love. 'Oooooooohm' …Christ Light, Christ Peace, etc."* over and over again.

I can't speak for the other guys but my only experience during this training session was a case of *"very sore knees."*

Apparently my brain became more relaxed than my body because during a moment of silence I unexpectedly yawned and Elvis responded with, *"Scuze me! Will ya please!"* To which everyone began to laugh, *"especially, Elvis."*

Seeing that I had single-handedly stopped the flow of all inspiration, Elvis reached down and picked up three small black books and gave one to each of us. It was a book on meditation entitled, *"The Impersonal Life."*

Inside the cover of each book, Elvis had written a personal comment to each of us. The note to me read, *"To Donnie: May 'The Light' give you warmth, protection and direction until you reach 'Home.' Friends forever, Elvis."*

Later that night, Elvis said he wanted to talk to me. I was quite uncertain as to what was about to happen but I followed him into his bedroom and together we sat down on the bed.

Within a short time Elvis began to talk about meditation and his need   to join with someone from whom he could draw spiritual reinforcement for his weakening inner man.

During our time together that evening, he never really shared with me the inward battle that he was having but I determined, from some of the comments that he made, that it was centered around his relationship with Priscilla and that he was seriously troubled over whatever his unstated thoughts were. At one point he said, ***"Man, I think I'm goin' off my rocker! It feels like 'I'm losing my marbles'!"***

To honor his request and really believing, at the time, that it would accomplish a positive reaction in his *"psyche,"* we both joined hands with his right hand in my left hand.

For a considerable period of time, we just sat there breathing slowly.

Some time later, with no other words spoken and with Elvis still in silence, I got up and quietly left him alone in his bedroom.

The next day, while shopping in Palm Springs with **"Ricky Stanley,"** Elvis' step-brother, I remembered a past moment, when Elvis gave me a box of marbles and at the same time I thought about the previous night. It was then that I had, what I thought was, a cool idea.

I found a little souvenir shop, went in and bought a very large and beautiful, crystal clear, aqua colored marble that cost about five dollars.

That night when we all got back together with Elvis, I waited until I could get to Elvis in a private moment and when the opportunity did arrive, I quietly said to him, ***"Boss! Ya remember how you said you felt last night?"*** He nodded his head and made a soft, ***"Um-huh"*** sound. I reached out with my closed hand and put into his hand the marble I had bought earlier that day, and I said to him, ***"Put this in ya pocket and hang tight. You 'da man and with this in ya pocket, you ain't never gonna lose 'em!"*** He smiled and we re- turned to the evening's festivities.

If I could snap my fingers and bring into existence all the things that I might wish for at this point in my life, there's one thing I would, for sure, snap into reality.

92

I would snap *"Elvis into today"* and at the age we would both be, it would be quite enjoyable for both of us to, suddenly find those glass orbs, from a time once lived, back in our possession again.

I like to think that, together, we just might duck out the back door of Graceland, run down into the horse pasture, find ourselves a little sandy spot, squat down and shoot a game:

With the
"marbles that we both lost"
once upon a _"real"_ long ago.

- Donnie Sumner

You Can't
"Wring Your Hands"
and
"Roll Up Your Sleeves"
At The Same Time

Choose To Be Happy

Kung Fu - R - Us

*E*lvis and I had a lot of opposites!

"He was handsome," I wasn't. *"He was rich,"* I wasn't. *"He was famous,"* I wasn't. *"He knew Karate"* and I didn't.

I always dreamed of being handsome, rich and famous but never at any time did I aspire for the strenuous discipline required to become proficient in the art of self-defense. Therefore, I became quite concerned when, during the summer of 1974, Elvis announced to all the men in my group, Voice, that he was going to teach us the art of Karate.

We were at Elvis' Palm Springs home and the members of my group,
Voice, *"Shaun Nielsen, Tim Baty"* and myself were swimming in *"the kings pool"* when *"Charlie Hodge"* stepped onto the patio and announced, *"The Boss wants to see y'all!"*

We climbed out of the pool, grabbed our towels, dried a little and proceeded into the house.

When we got inside the house, Elvis was standing in the middle of the living room dressed in his karate uniform and it was then that Elvis made the announcement that we were about to *"begin training."*

Elvis lined the three of us up and began to demonstrate various short katas, which were a series of moves resembling ballet movements. He then had each us to try duplicating them. I wasn't doing too badly until they got down to kicking.

Elvis made a mark on the wall for us to aim at and each of us were to try kicking the spot. Shaun was adequate. Tim was great! *"Ole Donnie,"* well, he never could get his foot higher than his waist!

When it came my turn to try, my effort landed way short of the goal. Not only did I miss the mark but I tried kickin' with so much force, I completely lost my balance and fell backwards. One second I was kickin' and the next I was sprawled out flat of my back on the floor. Elvis started laughing, jumped on top of my chest and began to act like he was giving me CPR.

It didn't take Elvis long to determine a truth, ***"You can't teach an unwilling dog a difficult trick!"***

After we had worked up a good sweat, Elvis called it a day and told each of us to create a personal kata for the next day. After much thought that night, this is the ***"D.H.S. self-protection kata"*** that I demonstrated to Elvis the next morning.

You stand sideways with your left leg and foot extended forward and firmly brace yourself in this ordinary defensive stance. Once this initial pose has been assumed, you slowly draw your left foot backward approximately two feet to bring it in line with your right foot. You follow that by slowly moving your right foot backward two or three steps. Once you are in balance, you repeat the same process again. After repeating this move three to four times, you abruptly turn your body one hundred eighty degrees and ***"run like crazy!"***

With that, Elvis fell to his knees and started laughin' really hard.

I always enjoyed making Elvis laugh.

- Donnie Sumner

Just like it raises
the corners of your mouth

A Good Laugh
Will Always
Lift Your Spirit

Joy Riding In Elvis' Convertible

J.D. Sumner, my uncle, was an *"antique"* car enthusiast.

For a number of years his *"pet prize"* was a 1932, pearl flaked, candy apple red Chevrolet with a Hurst transmission.

In 1972, while returning home from a west coast tour, The Stamps stopped at a Sonic Burger in Phoenix Arizona. The beautifully restored '32' Chevy was parked in a drive in cubical and it caught the attention of my Uncle Jake.

J. D. got off of the bus, walked over to the teenage driver and asked him how much he wanted for the car. To the amazement of all of us in the bus, the young man told him his price and J. D. came back into the bus, went into his back room, got the cash, went back out and paid the young fellow, on the spot. The young man then wrote out a bill of sale and I signed it as a witness. J. D. got back into the bus and The Stamps continued toward home with me following the bus, *"driving J. D.'s new toy."*

As we drove home that night, neither of us knew that our current excitement would one day be replaced by an even greater joy.

In 1974, The Stamps Quartet were all visiting with Elvis at Graceland. Elvis had asked J.D. to bring the group over to sing some *"Gospel music"* for him.

During our visit, Mr. Vernon Presley, Elvis' father, came in and told Elvis that he had brought his convertible around and that it was in the front driveway.

We all went outside and there in the driveway was a beautiful and *"shiny,"* 1964 red Lincoln convertible.

Elvis jumped in on the driver's side and told J.D. to get in. J.D. opened the passenger's door, slipped into his seat and then together, Elvis and J.D. proceeded to drive out through the gates of Graceland.

Sometime later, Charlie Hodge and I were sitting on the front stoop of the Graceland mansion when Elvis and J.D. drove back in. When they left earlier, Elvis was driving. Upon their return, J.D. was behind the steering wheel.

I walked up to the driver's side of the convertible and asked Uncle Jake what he was doing driving Elvis' car, to which he quickly responded, *"It ain't Elvis' car. It's mine!"*

I never knew, nor did I ever care, how much money was figured into the transaction but I feel confident that it was only a fraction of the actual value of the car. I am further confident that what ever the amount was, it was only accepted by Elvis at J.D.'s persistence. During the years I lived with Elvis, I came to understand the fact that he was a *"giver"* not a seller.

Soon after the return of Elvis and J.D., we all said our *"good byes"* and once again the Stamps were headed back to Nashville.

As we drove eastbound on Interstate 40, toward home, the driving duties of J.D. and myself had reversed. This time, I was riding on the bus and Uncle Jake was *"leading"* the convoy, driving his newly acquired *"red convertible, 'Elvis' chariot!"*

A couple of days after returning home, Uncle Jake invited me to go with with him to the airport hangar where his new car was being stored, along with his other cars. Once we arrived at the hangar, Uncle Jake got into the driver's seat of the convertible and told me to hop in. I did and then he proceeded to drive out onto Interstate 24 on the southeast side of Nashville.

As we headed south on the Interstate, I said to Uncle Jake, *"Let's see how fast she'll go boss!"* J.D. said back to me, *"You let me handle this. You just sit there and be Charlie, I'll be Elvis and we'll play a game called 'Shut Up and You're IT'!"*

I never got to drive Uncle Jake's crown jewel but I did produce a Stamps record entitled *"Vintage Gospel"* and I used a picture of The Stamps Quartet and J.D. sitting in it for the album cover.

I've often wondered what it must have felt like for Elvis or J.D. to go whippin' around town driving their:

"Big Red Continental Convertible."

I would have been thrilled!

But then:
"Wouldn't We All Have Been!"

- Donnie Sumner

Things always seem to end
and
you can't relive the past
but

Great Memories
LAST FOREVER!

My Faithful Four-Legged Friend

I spent a lot of childhood *"down time"* daydreaming about getting big and becoming a *"shoot-'em up"* cowboy.

In the late '40's and early '50's, my uncle, *"J.D. Sumner,"* was with the *"Sunshine Boys"* a *"western and gospel"* singing group. They were part of the cast starring in the old *"Durango Kid"* movie series. As far back as I can recall, I dreamed of being exactly like my *"Uncle Jake."*

I finally realized a tiny part of my dream during the eight years I was the lead vocalist for *"J.D. Sumner and The Stamps Quartet."*

For one week, in 1968, I got to ride on a horse playing the role of a young mountain man in the outdoor theatre  presentation of *"Shepherd Of The Hills"* in Branson, Missouri but I never did become a *"real"* cowboy. Other than my *"short"* acting role in Branson, the closest I ever got to a saddle was the one on an electric pony in front of a Wal Mart.

I don't know if Elvis ever dreamed of being a cowboy or if he just inherited his love of horses from some of the movie roles he portrayed but

I do know that he had some beautiful horses in the corral at Graceland.

I never rode a single one of Elvis' horses but I have stood, leaning on the corral fence, enjoying their beauty on numerous occcassions.

The last year I was with Elvis, I only spent twelve nights in my Nashville home. The remainder of the time, I was one of a small *"posse"* of men that was with Elvis constantly.

Being gone from your family for such an extended period of time will invariably create moments of *"great longing to see your kids."*

On numerous occasions, during a *"home attack,"* I would slip out of Elvis' Jungle Room door at Graceland, walk down to the pasture fence, stand there and wait for my four-legged *"shoulder to cry on"* to come up and nuzzle my hand.

I don't know his name, his breed nor his origin but I do know that he became my friend. He listened to every word I would speak, never asked any questions and never left before I did.

If he was prone to gossip . . .

He Sure Would Have Some Stories To Tell!

I don't know who Elvis'
"shoulder to cry on"
was:
But mine was:

*"A beautiful tan horse with loving eyes
and a long flowing mane"
who once lived at Graceland in Memphis, Tennessee."*

- Donnie Sumner

A Horse Makes
A Great Friend:

THEY WON'T TELL ON YA WHEN YA MESS UP!

A Springtime Gift

*I*t's hard to *"out rhinestone and embroidery"* Nashville, Tennessee's *"Grand Ole Opry"* but *"ELVIS DID!"*

The only custom made shirts I ever owned were those created and given to me by my friend, *"Elvis."* Most of my *"unusual"* shirts were for my stage apparel as a member my vocal group, *"Voice Inc:"* But three of those few shirts were worn as my *"everyday"* clothes and were, without a doubt, the fanciest *"duds"* that ever touched this ol' boys back.

One morning while we staying in Hollywood, Elvis decided he wanted to go shopping and I can assure you that *"shopping with Elvis"* was an enjoyable experience. The shopping entourage included; Elvis, Charlie Hodge, Red West, Ricky Stanley, Sean Nielsen, Tim Baty and myself. The limo was crowded when we started but was even less roomy on the way home. On our return trip, the limo was crammed, *"wall to wall"* with people and *"packages."*

When we arrived back at Elvis' Hollywood home on Monovale Drive, Elvis told Ricky and I to, *"Go put my stuff in my bedroom"* which is exactly what we proceeded to do. When we got into Elvis' bedroom we laid some of the things on the bed and I opened the closet to hang up Elvis' new jacket. I have never seen as many clothes in a closet in my life! Among the spectacle I was viewing, there were a large number of *"rhinestone and embroidered"* shirts neatly hanging on the end. I had previously been a member of the *"Grand Ole Opry"* and I had seen my share of *"glitz"* but never had I witnessed a collection like the one Elvis had.

Later that evening, while we were watching television in Elvis' den, I said to him, *"Boss, I saw your fancy shirts when I was hanging up your shoppin' stash this mornin'. When I get 'old' I'm gonna get me some shirts like that, go back to the 'Opry' and play like I'm Porter Wagoner on steroids."* Elvis responded with a hearty laugh.

In a couple of weeks, we were back at Graceland and one morning Elvis came downstairs with a box in his hand which he handed to me with a smile saying, *"Check this out."* Inside the box were three *"custom designed"* shirts just like some of the ones in his personal closet.

"Thank You!" is a short phrase but that is all I could come up with at the moment. Elvis smiled back at me and said, *"You ain't gotta be 'old' to be a star!"*

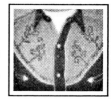

It's hard to *"eat breakfast, play all day and then sleep"* in a *"high dollar"* shirt but I managed to wear those puppies until the cleaners had knocked off most of the rhinestones and frayed a goodly portion of the embroidery.

But even *"worn out"* those were, without a doubt:

The Prettiest Shirts I Ever Owned!

- Donnie Sumner

A "true" friend is:
Hard To Find,
Difficult To Leave
and
IMPOSSIBLE TO FORGET!

Paper Doll Daddy

*V*ery few people have seen Elvis in his *"pajamas"* but I have.

"Keeper Of The Flames" was the nickname for one of my *"house"* duties when we were staying in Elvis' home on Monovale Drive in Hollywood.

I love the beauty of a blazing, open fireplace! Therefore, it was no coincidence that one of my Bel Air responsibilities was to maintain a glowing fire in the fireplace at all times, including the summer.

Elvis enjoyed using colored logs in his fireplace and the one in his Hollywood den was gigantic. On more than one occasion, I have been known to put as many as ten, Duraflame logs on the grate at one time. Needless to say, the multi-colored flames were always a spectacle to see.

It was my usual *"morning"* routine to get to the den before Elvis got there in order to make sure that the fireplace flames were in full color when he arrived.

In the spring of 1974, Elvis flew all of us to Hollywood for a short stay. One morning during this particular visit, I was preparing to begin my morning routine and was about to enter the den when I heard voices coming from inside the room.

I had no idea who it was or what was going on but my observation that morning is a memory that I truly wish every fan of Elvis could have shared with me.

When I finally ventured into the room, I observed that someone had stoked the fire and it was already showering radiant colors.

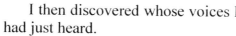

I then discovered whose voices I had just heard.

There was *Elvis and Lisa Marie:* sitting alone in the middle of the den floor.

Lisa Marie was dressed in a long nightshirt and Elvis was donned in a pair of dark blue, silk pajamas with white accent stripes. He had not yet shaven and his hair was n extreme disarray. He was a mess to see but it will *"always"* be one of *"my most treasured memories"* of him.

They were just sitting there like two kids around a campfire and hey were surrounded by what appeared to be an abundance of little bits and pieces of paper.

Can I be so bold as to tell you what the *"King of Rock,"* the *"Idol of Millions"* was doing that morning?

He was *"cuttin' out paper dolls!"*

The best part was when I noticed that he was using Lisa Marie's, *"little plastic scissors!"*

There was *"Daddy Elvis,"* a man who could buy dozens of gold plated shears, using a pair of *"fifty cent, plastic scissors"* just to please his *"little girl!"*

The *"world"* remembers, Elvis *"The Star,"* Elvis *"The King"* and numerous other *"Elvises"* of their own choosing but when I recall *"my"* memories of Elvis, that of *"the paper doll daddy"* stands out as one of my fondest.

"No one will ever be able to alter any of my remembrances of Elvis and I have 'nothing' negative to say about my friend, regardless of his human frailties!"

"He was a good, gracious and kind man!" I know! I lived with him! I worked with Him! I buddied with Him! Furthermore, I've been where very few have stood.

I have seen *"Elvis, The Loving Daddy!"*

- Donnie Sumner

No man stands so big
as one
who reaches out

To Touch The Hand
Of A Child

"Memories"

Memories,
pressed between the pages
of my mind.

Memories,
sweetened thru the ages
just like wine.

Quiet thought come floating down
And settle softly to the ground;

Like golden autumn leaves around my feet,
I touched them and they burst apart with
Sweet Memories:

Sweet Memories.

From:
Elvis' "68" Live Comeback Album

Part Of The Family

I guess you might say, *"Elvis, sorta sneaked up on me!"*

In the early 70's, I had retired from touring with my gospel group, *"The Singing Americans"* and had taken a position as the executive director of *"J.D. Sumner's"* artist management service known as the *"Sumar Talent Agency."*

Early in 1974, the baritone singer for *"J.D. Sumner and The Stamps Quartet,"* resigned his position and initiated his own solo career. With a vacant spot in The Stamps Quartet, J.D. asked me to fill in as his *"baritone"* until he could find a suitable voice for that vocal part.

A month or so went by and suddenly, one day, J.D. said to me, *"Ed, don't plan on going back to the office, you are now the baritone singer for The Stamps Quartet."*

I was even more surprised when J.D. added, *"We have an Elvis Tour in about a month, so, learn all the songs."*

I had never sung anything except Southern Gospel and the thought of singing with *"Elvis"* sorta made my head spin a little.

After returning to the reality of the moment, I said to J.D., *"How in the world am I gonna do that?"* J.D.'s response was to hand me Elvis' album, *"Live At Madison Square Garden"* with the comment, *"Listen to this and learn 'em just like we did 'em there and by the time we go on tour, you'll be ready!"*

To some, that would appear to be a small task but for an *"office oriented"* gospel singer, it promised to be a monumental task. For that reason, it was no coincidence that, every time anyone saw me for the next

few weeks, they were also greeted by my headphones with me listening to *"Elvis!"*

Looking back on it now, I can say that I experienced, both the discipline and the reward of being an *"old dog learnin' new tricks!"* I soon developed the ability to *"Ooh, Ah and Bop da Wah Da Wah"* just like the rest of the guys in the Stamps Quartet and until Elvis' death in 1977 that was what I did.

The day eventually came for me to begin my first tour with Elvis and during our flight to Los Angeles, J.D. casually said to me, *"Eddie, my boy, when we get to 'Elvis' house,' just treat 'him' like one of the guys."* I thought to myself, *"It's hard for me to do 'that' with some of my heroes in gospel music. How in the heck am I gonna pull it off with someone like 'Elvis'?"* It was that thought that caused me to ask J.D., *"How in the world do you treat a 'superstar like Elvis' as just 'one of the guys'?"* J.D. said back to me, *"Just do it! That's exactly the way he wants to be treated."* Again, I thought to myself, *"Eddie, ole boy, you got your work cut out for ya now!"*

J.D. went on to say, *"One more thing is really important. When we're on stage, keep your eyes glued to Elvis, 'cause ya never know what he might want ya to do."* He then added, *"Elvis is very aware of everything and everybody while he's in concert and if somebody messes up he's the first to know it!"* I thought, *"Great! I've got this part made; 'Cause I can mess up with the best of 'em!"*

May 10, 1974, finally arrived and I found myself at the Swing Auditorium in San Bernardino, California, *"live and on stage with 'Elvis Presley'!"* This short space will not allow me the luxury of describing the joy I was feeling!

During that first concert with Elvis, I began to notice that, more than frequently, he would look across the stage and fix his eyes on the Stamps Quartet and I kept thinking to myself, *"Oh Lord, it's me! I'm messin' up!"* Under the circumstances, I can assure you that such a thought can be quite unnerving, to say the least.

My fears were removed when, about half way thru the show, Elvis came over to the background vocalists, stuck his hand between the girls, took my hand and said, *"Welcome to the show, Ed!"* That, my friend, made me feel like I had just won the lottery.

Elvis was a master at knowing his entourage and his joy was doing things for them that would cause them to feel that they were truly important. It was his belief that this would make a great artist an even better artist. Elvis continually showed his loyalty and devotion to his friends that supported him on stage.

Little did I realize that first night in concert with Elvis, that I would soon live one of my fondest memories of Elvis' friendship.

Our tour was scheduled from June 15, 1974 thru July 2, 1974 and one of the venues was in Columbus, Ohio on the evening of June 25, 1974.

On that particular night, *"The Sweet Inspirations"* and *"Jackie Kahane"* had finished their part of the Elvis show and we were taking our usual intermission, at which point, Elvis and his bodyguards would always drive into the auditorium, park in a secure spot and then head immediately to Elvis' dressing room.

It was an unexpected surprise when Elvis' bodyguards approached me and said, *"Elvis wants to see ya!"* As usual, I thought to myself, *"Sakes alive! What have I done now?"*

When I arrived at Elvis' dressing room, I nervously entered and once inside, Elvis walked over to me and handed me a small black velvet case. With shaky hands, I opened the box and there inside it was a beautiful 14K gold necklace fashioned in the shape of a lightning bolt bearing the initials *"T.C.B."* across the top of it.

Elvis came closer to me and said, *"I'm gonna put it on ya and hug ya but I ain't gonna kiss ya!"* As usual, when Elvis did something unexpectedly, everyone had a hearty laugh.

I have never felt more special than when Elvis put my *"T.C.B."* around my neck, hugged me and said, *"Welcome To The Family!"*

From that time until his death in 1977, Elvis always made sure that I felt like:

"Part Of The Family!"

- Ed Hill

Memories warm you: From the inside.

Ladies and Gentlemen!

*W*hen you pick up the phone and the voice on the other end says, *"Hey man, this is Elvis!"* now that's both a shock and a pleasant surprise.

On the other-hand, when the voice you hear says, *"Good mornin' Ed, this is 'The Colonel',"* it is only a shock because your first thought would be, *"Oh Lord! I'm gonna be fired!"*

I can only imagine what J.D.'s thoughts might have been the day I was present when he received a phone call from Col. Parker, Elvis' manager.

In early September of 1994, I was talking with *"J.D. Sumner,"* my friend and boss, when his phone rang and the caller was Col. Tom Parker. The Colonel informed J.D. that they were gonna have to find a new announcer for Elvis' upcoming tour.

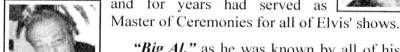

"Al Dvorin," a lifelong friend of the Colonel's, was head of all the show concessions and for years had served as Master of Ceremonies for all of Elvis' shows.

"Big Al," as he was known by all of his friends, also served the Colonel in the same positions on all of *"John Denver's"* shows. The Colonel had come into a situation where Elvis and John Denver had tours scheduled to run on the same days. Col. Parker had told Big Al to go ahead and tour with Denver and he would get a replacement for the Elvis tour.

When the entire situation had been presented to J.D., he immediately volunteered for *"me"* to fill in and do *"Big Al's job."*

Naturally, I joyfully accepted the responsibility. I only had one request: I didn't want to do it on stage in the manner that Big Al had always done it due to the fact that I was a member of *"The Stamps Quartet"* and we were the opening act. I didn't want to walk on stage announcing *"myself."* I wanted to do it from behind the stage so I could finish announcing and then enter with The Stamps, without looking out of place or awkward. They agreed that this would work and in a few days, I was *"off and running."*

My first tour as announcer seemed to go very well. However, what seemed to be *"going good"* from my perception, might not please Col. Tom. Furthermore, we all knew who had the final decision in all *"Elvis matters."*

The next morning, after we had boarded our plane and were headed to our next venue, *"Felton Jarvis,"* Elvis' R.C.A. record producer, leaned over my shoulder and said to me, *"You are now 'The official Elvis Tour Announcer.' Col. Tom liked the way you did it."*

It suddenly felt like a big truck had been lifted off my shoulders and I must admit, *"my chest swelled a little"* with joy. In jest I enjoy telling people, *"The Colonel sure is a great judge of talent. He hired both 'Me and Elvis'."*

From that first show until Elvis' death in 1977, I announced the selling of all Elvis souvenir items and introduced "*J.D. And The Stamps Quartet, The Sweet Inspirations"* as-well-as our comedian, "*Jackie Kahane*." One of my favorite announcements was the invitation to take an *"intermission."* That meant that I had time to go get a *"hot dog."*

Being back stage and in the dark, afforded my friends numerous opportunities to pull pranks on me and those times were considerable.

One night I was about to introduce The Stamps Quartet and I was enjoying the anticipation of walking onto another Elvis stage with J.D. and the guys, when silently in the darkness, someone slipped up behind me, pushed a big brown bag down over my head and starting pulling my coat off of me. After abruptly stopping my announcing, I thought to myself, *"Dear Lord! I'm about to go on stage and I'm being turned into naked mess!"*

When the bag was removed and I was able to understand what was happening, I turned around to determine the identity of my assailant. Wouldn't you know it! *"It was Elvis!"* He was laughin' so loud and so hard, everyone backstage heard it and proceeded to come over to join in the frivolity. Sometimes I remember the event and wonder if the audience, while hearing the laughter over the speaker system, thought that it coming was from me. *"It wasn't"* It was the hilarious laughter of *"My Friend, Elvis!"*

I still get chill bumps when I remember all the nights that I stood at the bottom of the stage steps and watched Elvis come rushing down. He would always smile at me, pat me on the shoulder and then as he was getting into his limo, shout out, *"Hey man! I'll see ya in a minute."*

Then as the *"T.C.B. Band"* and the orchestra continued playing the show's closing vamp, I would also make the famous closing announcement: *"Ladies and Gentlemen, Elvis has left the building. Thank you and good night."*

During a conversation I recently had with *"Donnie Sumner,"* the lead vocalist for both *"The Stamps Quartet"* and his own group *"Voice,"* he made this statement to me, *"Eddie, my boy, J.D.'s not here to say it but I can speak for him and I both when I tell ya that your 'Ladies and Gentlemen' line made history, Brother."*

I enjoy a lot of pleasurable moments remembering some of the joys I experienced in my role as the *"show announcer."* On the other-hand, I am often saddened remembering that in reality:

"My friend, 'Elvis' ... really has 'Left The Building'!"

- *Ed Hill*

Yesterdays Realities
are Todays Memories.
Only God Knows
What Tomorrow Will Bring.
Be Happy Today!

Same Song – New Stage

*W*ash ya face! Brush ya teeth! Get dressed! Ooh and Ah for a bit! Change clothes! Get on the bus and exit the venue!

To some, it may sound less than exciting but as for me: I never lost the thrill of those three or four hours that made up our evenings *"on tour with Elvis."*

As was our norm, after the July 20, 1975 show in Norfolk, VA, all of the cast changed into our casual attire, got on the show bus and headed back to our hotel.

As usual, the first thing I did was hit the hotel restaurant, where I was enjoying some *"less than home cooked"* food when one of Elvis' bodyguards came up to my table and said, *"Elvis wants to see all The Stamps."* So, once again, I followed the protocol for everyone associated with Elvis, *"When Elvis calls you go!"* I wiped my greasy mouth, stood up and left the restaurant, in order to join up with all of the other guys so we could answer our summons from Elvis.

Once we were all together, I, along with *"J.D. Sumner"* and all the rest of *"The Stamps,"* headed for Elvis' suite to see what he desired of us.

Upon our arrival, Elvis hugged each of us and then looking at J.D., he said, *"I've wanted to do something for a long time and now's the time to do it!"* I wondered to myself, *"Is he gonna shoot us or what!"* It was both a relief and a shock when he said to J.D., *"I want The Stamps to open my show from now!"* I don't know about all of the other guys but for me personally, you could have knocked me over with a feather.

To our amazement, Elvis reached out and gave each member of The Stamps Quartet a very healthy *"bonus check."* Upon viewing the gift, each of us was humbled by Elvis' gesture of friendship. The gift was not to persuade us to accept the offer to open his show; it was simply a *"friend"* being *"kind"* to *"another friend."*

Having been closely associated with Elvis for a significant amount of time, I can share with you an *"irrefutable fact:"* among all the pleasures at Elvis' disposal, *"his greatest joy was in the giving of meaningful gifts to those whom he loved."*

I was the recipient of numerous gifts from my friend Elvis and each of them was humbly received and greatly appreciated but the real asset was not in the gift, it was in the loving *"friendship"* of *"The Giver."*

The *"Good Book"* declares, *"Unto whom much is given, much is required."*

Consequently, once the reality of The Stamps *"new role"* finally dawned on us, we were faced with a small problem. *"What in the world*

are we gonna sing?" Each of us gave J.D. our individual thoughts and suggested a variety of songs, none of which were gospel. J.D. patiently listened to all of his *"musical advisers"* and when each of us had exhausted our knowledge and expertise, J.D. quietly said, *"Those are all great songs fellows but I've been a 'gospel singer' for nearly fifty years and I'm too old to change now so, here's what we're gonna do. We gonna sing 'Southern Gospel'!"*

Once again, J.D.'s experience and insight proved to be right. Lookin' back on it now, I can't imagine me suggesting anything other than a *"gospel"* tune because, like J.D., that's the only kind of music I have ever sung. My wife Sharon often reminds me of that fact when she says, *"You would have made a lousy Frank Sinatra or Michael Jackson but you sure are a great gospel singer!"* In the privacy of my own mind I sometimes think, *"I sure hope she's right!"*

I am grateful that J.D. did not stray from his gospel roots because the mutual love for Gospel Music between Elvis and J.D. became another point of contact that brought them even closer together.

I enjoyed a lot of *"firsts"* during my years with Elvis but I would have to place the night of July 21, 1975 within the section of those *"most memorable."* That was the night that *"J.D. Sumner and The Stamps Quartet"* had the joyful privilege of opening our first concert for Elvis.

The Stamps had delivered numerous *"Gospel"* concerts in Greensboro, NC and our fans in that city had always been extremely supportive of our music but this particular concert was promising to be a great deal different than those we had done in the past.

In just a few minutes, we were gonna be the *"opening act"* for *"Elvis Presley, The King of Rock and Roll!"*

I can't speak for the other guys in The Stamps but I can tell you, for sure, that when the stage manager came into our dressing room and announced, *"Showtime in fifteen minutes!"* I got as nervous as a cat in a room full of rockin' chairs.

I looked at my watch. It said, *"Eight O'clock P.M."* I heard *"Al Dvorin,"* our show announcer, say through the sound system, *"Good evening Ladies and Gentlemen. Welcome to the Elvis Presley Show. Here to begin tonight's performance, would you welcome to our stage, J.D. Sumner and The Stamps Quartet!"* That's when I did exactly what you would have done: *"I nearly fainted from the excitement!"*

I am still amazed at how well we were received by the Elvis fans and how many of them have remained our friends through all these years. May I say, *"Thank you for the privilege of being able to call you 'our friend!'."*

From that premier performance until our very last concert with Elvis, *"Gospel Music,"* as performed by *"J.D. Sumner and The Stamps Quartet,"* was a standard part of the *"Elvis Presley show."*

I am still in awe at how an 'ole boy from the hills of Tennessee ever became blessed enough to be able to tell, *"The Greatest Story Ever Told;"* sharing the same stage with:

"The Greatest Entertainer That Ever Lived!"

- Ed Hill

I am just and ordinary man
who has been blessed
with extraordinary opportunities!

Songs, Gifts and Laughs

*M*ost artists go to a *"sound studio"* to create their recorded music but, then again, *"Elvis is not most artists."*

The studio *"comes to him!"*

Having recorded at every major sound facility in the country, Elvis eventually became very bored with going into a recording studio and enduring the inconvenience of making music in an atmosphere that did not heighten his enthusiasm. It is no wonder that Elvis chose to record his last few projects in the luxury of *"Graceland's jungle room."*

On one occasion, I overheard a conversation between Elvis and his friend *"Charlie Hodge."* Charlie was explaining to Elvis that *"Joe Esposito,"* Elvis' chief aid, had received a phone call from *"Colonel Tom Parker,"* Elvis' manager, stating that his contract with R.C.A. required him to have an audio master *"in house"* within just a few days. I heard Elvis answer Charlie with, *"Well, tell 'em if they want one, then come to 'the house' and get it!"* And that, boys and girls, is exactly what R.C.A. did from that time forward.

I wish you could have been there during one of those *"Graceland"* recording sessions. You would have been privy to a much more crowded scene than that what is visible today. When everyone got assembled, there were cars parked almost to the front gate and the entire side area parking, as well as the back parking portion of Graceland, was filled with big transport trucks. If you would have come inside the mansion proper, you would have been greeted with multiple, large moving cases, scattered all over the place.

Standing amid all the exaggerated clutter you would invariably be thrilled by the same scene that always excited me: *"Elvis,"* relaxing in his *"special chair"* in the jungle room, wearing his *"less than conventional"* attire, holding a microphone and laughing at something Charlie Hodge had just said or done.

In 1976, I experienced one of those times.

Elvis had been called on for a new R.C.A. record and all of the instrumentalist and singers had congregated at Graceland and we were all awaiting the opportunity to, once again, share the music of our mutual friend *"Elvis!"*

It seemed that, in his own mind, Elvis assumed that his voice was *"too raspy"* and for two full nights and three days everyone just had a *"good time,"* hanging out and enjoying *"Elvis."*

The first night *"Red West,"* one of Elvis' bodyguards, came into the *"jungle room"* with a big box of demos from various writers and we all sat around listening to songs for Elvis to choose from.

The next evening, Elvis still didn't feel like recording and he proceeded to have a *"give-away"* party. For quite a long period of time, Elvis had Red West bringing clothes galore into the den. I was absolutely amazed at all the shirts, jackets, slacks and long coats that kept coming thru the door. Most of them were brand new but a portion of them were taken directly from Elvis' personal wardrobe. When we all started to leave that night, it looked like the checkout line at Macy's.

In the afternoon of the third day, Elvis made the announcement, *"My voice ain't in no shape to record right now, so, we're calling off the session and we'll get back together in a few days."* He went on to say, *"I'm gonna get each of ya a 'limo' to take ya home."* A couple of the guys were from Nashville and they told Elvis that they lived close to each other and one limo would be fine for them.

To know Elvis means that you also know, *"One of anything is never enough!"* It was, therefore, no surprise when Elvis answered them back with, *"No! I want everybody to have their own limo!"*

Elvis then turned to J.D. and gave him a real shock when he said to him, *"J.D., I'm getting ready to get myself a new limo so I'm gonna give you the one I have now, as a gift. You and the boys have fun on the way home."*

Later that night, Elvis walked with us to J.D.'s *"new chariot"* as we prepared to leave. After he hugged J.D., Elvis took off the *"tan Shazam hat"* that he was wearing and popped it onto the head of J.D.

saying, *"Wear this J.D! It might improve your image!"* As usual we all laughed.

As we headed eastbound on Interstate 40, toward Nashville, J.D. was in the driver's seat, still wearing his new hat and I was in the backseat savoring the moment. I couldn't see J.D.'s face but in all probability, it was showing one of the biggest grins one could ever imagine.

Several days later, J.D. called me and said he was coming by to pick me up so that we could pick up my daughter, Lisa, after school in *"Elvis' limousine."* When J.D. arrived, he was wearing a black chauffeur's hat that he had purchased especially for Lisa's ride. He gave me Elvis' tan Shazaam hat, told me to put it on and get in the back seat. I did, and we headed off to pick up Lisa.

Lisa was not the only one surprised by the event. Both, J.D. and I were equally surprised when, a few days later, Lisa informed us that all of her friends at school were telling everybody that Elvis had come by to pick her up in his limousine.

Most folks would not admit that I *"look like Elvis"*

But there are a few kids who think, I do!

- Ed Hill

Humor isn't for everybody:
It's reserved for those
Who want to Enjoy Life.

Things Happen

*I*t has been said that, *"If anything can go wrong: It will!"*

I have been the recipient of that truth on numerous occasions. Therefore, I am no stranger to inconvenience and as a rule, I just *"go with the flow."* On the other hand, *"J.D. Sumner,"* my friend and boss, was a different story altogether.

J.D. was one of the most gentle and kind hearted friends I have ever had the pleasure to know and I'm not certain if it was his six foot, six inch

height or his awesomely low speaking voice but to someone unfamiliar with J.D., he might come across as a *"grizzly bear"* when they encountered him for the first time. In addition to his *"intimidating persona,"* J.D. could handle any situation with *"great ease."* He had the unique ability of taking an unpleasant situation and turning it into a humorous event that would be well worth remembering.

I can recall a large number of occurrences that J.D. made memorable, using his *"only J.D. could get by with it"* response to the unexpected.

One such event took place on June 25, 1977, in Cincinnati, Ohio.

We were on tour with Elvis and we were to stay at the Downtown Hilton in Cincinnati. When the full cast of *"The Elvis Show"* invaded a hotel lobby, we all acted like a bunch of monkeys with new wrist watches and the Hilton in Cincinnati was no different.

It seemed that all was going as well as could be expected until J.D. was finally able to get to the front desk for his turn to register. As was the custom when a guest was checking in, the hotel desk clerk asked J.D. for his name. In his extremely low bass voice he said, *"J.D. Sumner."* The

 clerk began going thru the hotel files and after a moment said to J.D., *"I'm sorry, Mr. Sumner. We don't show a reservation in your name. Are you certain that you are at the correct hotel?"*

If I had been in the same situation, in all probability, I would still be Cincinnati awaiting trial for disturbing the peace but, once again, J.D. came through like a champ.

Answering back in his lowest voice, J.D. said to the clerk, *"In that case, just have someone bring a pillow and a blanket and leave them here in the lobby. I'll be back down, in just a minute. I'm the 'bass singer' with the 'Elvis Presley Show' and I need to go up to 'Elvis' room' and let him know that if he needs me before tonight, I'll be down here in the lobby taking a nap!"* The laughter of *"Estelle Brown"* and *"Sylvia Shemwell,"* both from the *"Sweet Inspirations,"* could have probably been heard down in the next block.

You already know the ending, I'm sure! In less than a few minutes, J.D. was securely situated in a room that, only a short while ago, was unavailable!

May I remind you again that, *"Sometimes, things happen!"* J.D. was *"not the only one"* with *"hotel problems"* that day!

Later that same afternoon, I went downstairs to join the rest of the crew for our bus ride to Riverfront Stadium to do our daily sound check. When I got to the lobby, I saw something that I had never seen before.

"Elvis" was sitting at the front door, surrounded by his personal staff and his bodyguards. That scene was most unusual, to say the least.

After questioning *"Red and Sonny West,"* Elvis' bodyguards, as to the reason they were all in the lobby, I received the following information.

For some unknown reason, the air conditioning unit had stopped working in Elvis' room and he was getting really uncomfortable. Elvis and all of his personal entourage where waiting for a limousine to take them to another hotel. The interesting part is: *"The new hotel was only a half block down the street!"* Elvis never enjoyed waiting on anything and very shortly he decided he wasn't going to wait any longer for the limo and said, *"Come on! We'll walk!"*

A lot of Elvis' fans were not able to secure tickets for his show that night and I have always wondered what it might have been like for some big fan of Elvis, with no hope of seeing him in person, were to suddenly look up and see, *"The King Of Rock and Roll,"* casually walking along the side-walk, smiling and waving at passers-by.

For security while on tour, *"Colonel Parker,"* Elvis' manager, always reserved for Elvis, the top floor of each hotel in which he was to stay. A great portion of the time, there were far more rooms on that floor than Elvis' personal entourage could fill.

When there were enough vacant rooms on Elvis' floor, he always asked *"J.D. and The Stamps Quartet"* to stay with him on *"his"* floor.

It was not unusual for us to leave our doors open on such occasions because the security force was well able to keep anyone from getting onto the floor without an invitation. Nor was it unusual to be sitting in your room watching television and one your friends, just walk right in, unannounced, sit down and begin a conversation.

I was relaxing in my room one afternoon, when in walked *"Elvis."* It took me completely by surprise because Elvis had never been to any of my rooms in the past. I was even more astonished when he went over to my bed, plopped down on it and said, *"I just 'love' southern Gospel music!"*

Beginning with that comment, we went on to share a lengthy conversation about the *"southern Gospel"* genre and the host of southern Gospel artists that had affected his life. I was amazed at Elvis' overall knowledge of the gospel music industry and all the gospel friends we had in common. We must have talked for at least an hour and then he simply stood up and said, *"Gotta' go! See ya tonight. Take care. Love all you guys!"*

I can truthfully state for the record that, while on tour with Elvis, every day was truly a fresh adventure and sometimes unusual things happened. The good news is . . . *With Elvis:*

"It always turned out to be a beautiful memory!"

- Ed Hill

If there were no rocks in the water: You couldn't enjoy the sound of A Babbling Brook!

Happy Tracks In The Cow Pasture

*E*lvis loved to give gifts. He was one of the most giving men one could ever call their friend.

More than frequently, Elvis showered lavish gifts upon everyone that worked with him and as part of his inner circle, I was often on the receiving end of his generosity.

I think I can speak for all of us who called Elvis, *"friend,"* when I say; *"All of us were extremely grateful for the elegant gestures of thanks he extended to us individually but the warmth was not in the gifts, but rather, in the love with which they were given. Elvis truly cared for everyone in his 'T.C.B. Family'."*

"Elvis" and *"J.D. Sumner"* were closer than brothers and it always appeared to me that Elvis had an insatiable desire to flood J.D. with grandiose gifts. The *Elvis and Hollywood Legends Museum*, in *Pigeon Forge, Tennessee,* has on display a large quantity of the elaborate jewelry that Elvis gave to J.D. through the years.

There was one particular gift that Elvis gave to J.D. that is far too big to fit within the confines of a museum showcase. Let me tell you about *"The T.C.B. Bus."*

J.D. Sumner was the father of what has become known as the *"Celebrity Touring Bus."*

In 1955, J.D. was the bass singer for a singing group known as, *"The Sunshine Boys,"* who were co-headliners on Wheeling, West Virginia's, *"W.W.V.A. Jamboree,"* a sister broadcast of Nashville, Tennessee's *"Grand Ole Opry."*

Earlier that same year, a Memphis, Tennessee based southern Gospel quartet billed as *"The Blackwood Brothers Quartet,"* had endured a tragic accident. Their private, twin engine, Beechcraft plane had crashed in Clanton, Alabama and two members of their group were killed.

Shortly after the loss of R.W. Blackwood, the quartet's baritone singer, and Bill Lyles, their bass, *"James Blackwood,"* manager and owner of The Blackwood Brothers Quartet, contacted J.D. in regard to filling the, now vacant, position of bass singer for the group. J.D. accepted the offer of James and became a full partner with him in all Blackwood Enterprises.

The group had chosen not to fly any longer and they were touring in a seven passenger, Cadillac limousine. J.D., standing six foot, six inches tall, found long hours, for days on end, cooped up in a car with four other guys, very uncomfortable. One day J.D. announced to the group that he had just bought a used bus and was putting together a company (*later to become known*  *as "Crown Interiors"*) to outfit the bus interior similar to the design of a passenger train's *"pull-man car"* Very soon the The Blackwood Brothers Quartet were commuting cross country with all the comforts of home at their disposal.

Other gospel groups liked the idea and within a short time J.D.'s custom interior company had outfitted several buses for various southern Gospel Quartet's.

That first bus of J.D.'s started the industry now known as *"celebrity tour bus leasing."* It seems that now-a-days, the first prerequisite for a successful music career is the ownership of a *"mega buck,"* custom designed tour bus.

In 1976, J.D. had ordered a *"brand new"* MCI bus for The Stamps Quartet and was in the process of finalizing the purchase procedure. While on tour with Elvis during that time period, J.D. was enthusiastically discussing this new bus with Elvis.

J.D. learned a lesson that day: **With Elvis, "Don't mention it unless you've already paid for it."**

While they were talking, Elvis went over to a night stand drawer, pulled out a checkbook, handed it to J.D. and said, *"Write out a check out for whatever the price of the bus is and I'll sign it!"* If I had been told to write a check to myself from Elvis' personal checking account, I'm not certain what the amount would have been but J.D.'s reply was *"No way* 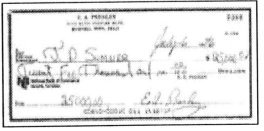 *man! I can't do that!"* Elvis came back with, *"You can write can't 'cha!"* J.D.'s answer was *"Of course I can write but I'm not gonna do ya that way!"* Elvis finally said to J.D., *"You're gonna have that new bus 'cause I'm gonna see to it!"* True to his word, Elvis *"saw to it"* with a check sent by mail to J.D. for *$25,000.00*.

In a few weeks J.D.'s interior design company had completed its work and J.D., along with all the Stamps, headed for Memphis to show the bus to Elvis and share our joy with him. Three hours later, a forty foot, orange and white MCI bus with a large *"T.C.B."* insignia on the side, was sitting in the driveway at *"Graceland's front doors."*

Upon our arrival, Elvis and his very close friend, *"Charlie Hodge,"* met us and came inside the bus to look at its elaborate interior. Once Elvis had seen all the amenities of the new *"T.C.B. Chariot,"* he wanted to drive it and *"drive it, he did!"*

Elvis got behind the steering wheel, cranked up the bus and started down his driveway toward *"Elvis Presley Boulevard."* At that time, most of the land directly in front of Graceland was an unfenced cow pasture and the average person, upon leaving the gates of Graceland, would have turned either left or right onto Elvis Presley Boulevard. *Not so with Elvis!* Elvis proceeded to drive across the highway, *"right out into the cow pasture"* and then he floored the accelerator and hollered, *"Hey, J.D.! Let's see what kind'a pick up she's got!"*

I don't know if you've ever been on a forty foot bus speeding thru a cow pasture but I can assure you, from experience, that it is more than a rough ride and after several hard jolts, J.D. hollered out to Elvis, *"Ya better slow this thing down, ya gonna tear the bottom out of it."* Elvis' reply was simple and well stated, *"If I do, I'll buy ya another one!"*

I'm not certain as to when construction began on the many pavilions across the street from Graceland but I am most certain of one thing: When they poured their first concrete foundation, they most assuredly covered over a lot of:

"Happy Tracks!"

- Ed Hill

If you can't enjoy it, What's the use of having it!

Welcome To Water World

*I*f you ever saw Elvis holding a glass of water, *"you better get out of the way!"*

Elvis enjoyed laughing and he would do anything for a hearty chuckle. It seems that *"water"* was involved in his *"wacky pranks"* on more than one occasion.

There was never a dull moment singing on stage with Elvis. The backup vocalists not only had to pay close attention to what Elvis required musically but we also became very adept at keeping an eye out for what he might do to, intermittently, just to spark his own enthusiasm.

When *"Al Dvorin,"* our show announcer, chose to retire, *"Colonel Parker"* placed me in that position and from that point until Elvis' last performance, I was the emcee for the show. Not only did I welcome the fans, promote souvenir sales and introduce the groups but I was also very honored to be able to close each show with the famous line, *"Ladies and gentlemen, 'Elvis has left the building!' Thank you and goodnight."*

In order to make my evenings more comfortable, each night, Colonel Parker made arrangements for me to have an off-stage stool to sit on while I was awaiting my next announcement. Elvis would often arrive at the venue during, or just prior to, intermission. If per chance he should arrive early, it became his practice to wait until I was *"on stage"* making an announcement and, in the *"backstage darkness,"* sneak over to my *"off-stage stool"* and pour an entire glass of *"ice cold"* water on it, *"ice included."* At the conclusion of my announcements, it was my habit to walk backstage and plop down on my stool. Very often I was welcomed by a *"pant's bottom full of water."* To add insult to injury, as they say, I could always hear Elvis, somewhere off in the darkness, laughing his head off. In all probability, I would have laughed too if I could have seen how quickly I could get up from flooded stool and how aggressively I could wipe crushed ice from the seat of my britches.

One night, in jest, I told Elvis, *"The least you could do is leave me a diaper to change into!"* Knowing Elvis, I'm surprised that he never stopped one of his shows in order to present me with a carton of *"Baby Pampers!"*

Over in the hills of East Tennessee, where I was raised, I oft'times heard them use the saying: ***"You ain't even wet behind the ears yet!"*** That may have been so in my early years but it sure changed after I joined the ***"Elvis Show!"*** Not only was my ***"bottom"*** usually wet ***"before"*** Elvis began his performance but the ***"top"*** was often drenched ***"after"*** he hit the stage.

The very physical stage activities of Elvis, made it necessary for him to drink a large amount of liquids during a performance. For that reason, ***"Charlie Hodge,"*** Elvis' stage companion, kept a big supply of Gatorade and bottled spring water on his side of the stage and every time Elvis would walk near Charlie's spot, he would reach out and sip on a drink that Charlie had waiting for him.

As the shows progressed, Elvis began spending more and more time on the vocalists' side of the stage and eventually Charlie developed the routine of putting a glass of water under ***"my"*** seat on the vocal ensemble's stand. It became common for Elvis to come over to our side and ask ***"me"*** to give him a drink. Most of the time, it was during his introductions of the back-up personnel.

The first couple of times Elvis asked me for a drink during our introductions, in my rush to get the glass to him, I spilled a few drops of water and they landed on his hand. When those little drops of water touched his skin, Elvis would holler, ***"Oh!"*** It would always sound as if he had just been hit with liquid fire. I should have known that, ***"someday, someway,"*** he was gonna ***"get even"*** with me for getting his hand wet.

Shortly after the first couple of ***"accidental spills,"*** I became the ***"willing"*** victim of another ***"Elvis water adventure"*** that we soon came to expect. I would hand Elvis the glass, he would make his exaggerated ***"hurt"*** yell and after the laughter had subsided, continue on with the introductions, all the while, slowly sipping from the glass of water I had given him. When the introductions were concluded, Elvis would turn to walk back into the center of the stage, then abruptly turn around and throw the remaining bit of water in his glass, ***"onto to me.!"*** Elvis ***"baptized"*** me often.

I wasn't the only recipient of Elvis' ***"liquid comedy!"***

Of all the folks in our back-up ensemble that could both receive pranks and give them back, ***"Estelle Brown,"*** of ***"The Sweet In-***

spirations," was a prime candidate for the award.

During one particular performance, Elvis began singing, *"You've Lost That Loving Feeling."* As usual during that song, the stage lights went dark and Elvis' head came back to view in a cameo spotlight. Just before the lights would ordinary come back to a full stage cover, we all heard *"Estelle"* say, *"Good Lord, what in the world is that!"* As the lights came to full power, we saw in Elvis' hand, a *"water pistol"* and *"Estelle"* had just been *"shot!"* We all laughed along with Estelle, not knowing that she would soon get her revenge.

On the next show, Estelle made her comeback. As Elvis neared the ending of the song, *"Suspicious Minds,"* as usual, he began to demonstrate his karate skills as *"Ron Tutt,"* Elvis' drummer, accented all of Elvis' kicks and punches. At one spot during the exercise, Elvis always moved into a defensive position by raising his arms in a combat stance, squatting down on his right leg and then extending his, straightened, other leg as far to the left as he possibly could. When Elvis started the move of this particular show, he didn't know that Estelle 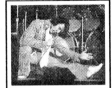 had been to the hotel gift shop between shows and had purchased four water pistols. One for herself, one for *"Kathy Westmoreland"* and two

 more for *"Myrna Smith* and *Sylvia Shemwell,"* both of *"The Sweet Inspirations."*

As every eye in the audience focused on the exciting pose that Elvis had gotten into, the girls, *"water brigade"* unleashed their arsenal. All four girls pulled out their water pistols, simultaneously aimed for and *"hit"* the crotch of Elvis's jump suit.

I have seen Elvis fake surprise on numerous occasions but I can recall one event by which he was genuinely startled:

The night that Elvis' *"blue suede shoes"* turned into *"water soaked trousers!"*

- Ed Hill

Joyful moments are never lost.
They will always come to life again;
When Remembered!

Hit The Water Boys!

I have sung in the rain, the snow, in sleet and hail and even in the desert but I never aspired to sing in a swimming pool. Never-the-less, *"I once did"* in Las Vegas, Nevada.

In 1975, during one of our Elvis engagements at the Hilton Hotel in Vegas, *"Rev. William Sharp,"* a local pastor and a minister friend of *"J.D. Sumner,"* was presenting a telethon on a Las Vegas television station in order to raise funds for a new church he wished to build. On three previous occasions, in another city, *"The Stamps Quartet"* had given performances for this same minister.

The telethon was being broadcast from the *"swimming pool"* pavilion atop the *"Landmark Hotel"* which stood directly across the street from the Las Vegas Hilton where Elvis and his entire entourage were staying. Because J.D. had been his friend for such a long time, the pastor felt comfortable in asking J.D. to bring The Stamps Quartet over to sing a song on his broadcast. When he was asked to do so, J.D. agreed to honor the preacher's request and promised him that we would come over and sing for him after our second Elvis show that night.

When Elvis was working in Las Vegas, The Stamps had a nightly routine. Each evening following our second show, we would all congregate in Elvis' suite on the twenty-eighth floor of the Hilton and sing *"Southern Gospel"* songs for him until he chose to *"call it a day."*

Earlier that day, during our time with Elvis, he became aware of the fact that The Stamps were going to be singing on television that night. Elvis loved to hear Gospel music by The Stamps and apparently didn't want to miss our singing simply because it wasn't going to be created in his suite because he had *"Joe Espisito,"* his personal aide, to call *"The Sweet Inspirations, Kathy Westmoreland,"* as-well-as the *"T.C.B. Band"* and have them all come up to his suite after the second show because, *"We're gonna watch The Stamps on T.V. Tonight!"*

When the The Stamps were with Elvis in Vegas, we only had the four vocalists. Our pianist usually had that time off and would remain in Nashville. *"Donnie Sumner,"* the nephew of J.D. Sumner and the former lead singer for The Stamps, now had his own group known as *"Voice."* His group lived with Elvis and sang with us on all of Elvis' shows and records.

Being a great keyboard man and so readily available, J.D. asked Donnie to go with us to The Landmark and play the piano. So, after Elvis' second show at the Hilton that night, The Stamps and Donnie, *"still dressed in our stage uniforms,"* all headed across the street to join *"the preacher."*

Once on the telethon set, the host introduced The Stamps to sing *"one song."* During our performance, one of the donation phones received an incoming call and on the other end of the line was *"Elvis."* We found out later that Elvis had said to the operator, *"This is Elvis Presley and I want The Stamps to sing some songs for me, so if you would, just stay on the line with me and I'll tell 'em what to sing."* The lady did what anyone else would have done when they were on the phone with Elvis: *"She stayed on line!"* As Elvis would give the assistant a song title, The Stamps would sing it. After a couple of songs, the operator informed the host that Elvis would donate *$1,000.00* if *"Bill Baize,"* the tenor for The Stamps, would sing *"When It's My Time."* We sang the request and did another song or two and the dear lady came over again and said that Elvis would donate another *$1,000.00* if *"Donnie"* would sing *"The Lighthouse."* Again, we honored Elvis' request and sang the song.

Not only was it exciting to be singing songs especially for Elvis but it was also a fun event because our stage backdrop was the beautiful swimming pool atop the Landmark Hotel. We were all enjoying the pleasures of the evening and for about another hour or so, Elvis continued calling out songs and we, in turn, sang each of them.

I can only imagine what must have been going on in Elvis' suite as we sang but I am certain that there must have been some laughter going on because, quite excited like, the phone attendant came over to *"the preacher"* and said to him, *"Mr. Presley said he would donate $2,000.00 dollars if 'The Stamps would jump into the swimming pool'."*

"What Elvis wants: Elvis gets!" Therefore, it did not come as a surprise when J.D. yelled out, *"Hit the water boys!"* And that, boys and girls, is exactly what we did; Head first we went, clothes, shoes, and wallets! Laughing just as hard as Elvis must have been laughing in his suite, the stage hands came over and helped pull us all out of the pool.

It's unusual to sing in *"soaked clothes"* but we managed to get started on another tune that Elvis had just requested.

Over in the *"dry luxury"* of his suite Elvis was probably laughing so hard that he couldn't hear the song we were singing because at the conclusion of the tune, the telethon attendant came over, stood beside J.D., and said to him, *"Mr. Presley wishes to speak with you."* Then she handed

the phone to J.D.

The exchange during that conversation soon became very evident. Elvis had told J.D. that he would give another *$2,500,00* if J.D. would *"throw 'The Preacher' into the pool."*

J.D. handed the phone back to the sweet lady and invited the Preacher to come over on our side of the stage set and join The Stamps. With a big smile, the minister rushed over to stand beside The Stamps. J.D. turned to him and said, *"Elvis told me he would give another $2,500.00 if we'd throw 'you' in the pool. So, my friend, get ready for your baptismal!"* Then with a big shove, J.D. pushed the Preacher, who was dressed in an all-white, custom made suit, into the swimming pool. Our minister friend wanted to make a *"big splash"* that night but I don't suspect that he had anticipated doing it in that manner.

When the telethon concluded, The Stamps went downstairs and as we reached the hotel lobby, we were met by a couple of Elvis' aides who had brought us coats to stay warm in while we rode back to the Hilton in limousines that Elvis had just provided for us. When we got back to the Hilton, *"Elvis,"* along with *"Dr. 'Nick',"* was waiting for us in his suite. When he saw us, he gave each of us a bathrobe and said, *"Put these on and go in the bedroom 'cause Dr. Nick's gonna give ya a B-12 shot so ya don't 'come down' with some-thing!"*

The next night, during our first show, as we were coming near the end of *"I Got a Woman,"* Elvis pointed to J.D., fully expecting him to hit the extremely low note on *"Amen"* that J.D. had become noted for. On *"that"* particular show, it was not to be so. Surprising himself, as-well-as all of us, J.D. *"flubbed the note, big time."* There was nothing wrong with his voice and there was no other reason for the blunder: J.D. just *"flat missed it!"*

As we were heading back to Elvis' suite after the show, Elvis jokingly said to J.D., *"Great job tonight on 'Amen' J.D.!"*

Not wanting to admit that there was no reason for the bad note and that there was absolutely nothing wrong with his throat, J.D. responded back to Elvis with the comment, ***"It must have been the cold pool last night. I've got a lot of 'congestion' in my lungs!"***

J.D. wished afterward that he had not ***"played sick"*** because as soon as we got upstairs, Elvis called ***"Dr. Elias Ghanem,"*** a close friend who was also a Las Vegas surgeon, and shortly thereafter, J.D. found himself laying on Elvis' bed, surrounded by medical devices, with Elvis and Dr. Ghanem inserting suction tubes into J.D.'s lungs, in an effort to remove the ***"non-existent congestion."***

Suffice it to say, The Stamps never did another telethon nor did J.D., ***"ever again,"*** create a phony excuse for any low note he might have missed.

My friends, ***"Elvis, Charlie and J.D."*** have now been joined together again for all eternity and down here on earth, I sometimes imagine them sittin' around on their golden sofas and laughin' about ***"throwing the preacher in the pool"***

and the night "Elvis played Doctor!"
- Ed Hill

Sometimes
The Bite
Is Worse Than The Bark!

Flyin' High

*D*id you ever fly on *"The Lisa Marie?"*

I've been asked that question a lot and the short answer is: *"Yes ... and ... often!"* I especially remember my first ride on the Lisa Marie. But first, let me tell you about the plane itself.

On April 17, 1975 Elvis bought a Convair 880 Jet, recently taken  out of service by Delta Airlines, for which he paid the *"then-substantial"* sum of *$250,000.00*. After re-furbishing the interior of the plane, the total cost exceeded *$600,000.00*. Upon purchasing the plane, Elvis immediately christened it as *"The Lisa Marie."*

Elvis put the plane in a hangar at Meacham Field in Fort Worth and for months he took great pleasure in flying friends out to check on the interior of the plane as it was being refurbished to  his very specific design requirements. It was customized with plush sleeping quarters, a pent-house bedroom with a custom-made queen size bed, an executive bathroom with gold faucets and a gold washbasin, a videotape system linked to four TVs and a stereo system with fifty-two speakers, an in-flight reading library and a conference room finished in teak wood. The plane could hold a maximum of 29 people, but usually there would be about eight or ten aboard. When the final paint job was applied to the exterior, Elvis had a prominent *"TCB"* logo stenciled onto the tail. Elvis was especially excited about the fact that the same design team had previously customized *"Air Force One."* When the plane was finished it was an air-worthy version of Graceland's elegance.

In November of 1975, when the plane was finally ready for service,  I was in Las Vegas working with Elvis at the Las Vegas Hilton. One night after our second show, Elvis came into the Stamps dressing room and said, *"Hey guys, I want 'cha to go with me to see my new plane."* To which J.D. Sumner promptly replied, *"Great!"* The Lisa Marie had been delivered to the airport in Las Vegas and with Elvis's limo in the lead and two more limo's following close behind, we all headed to the air field. When we arrived beside the plane, Elvis invited us all to come aboard and see the *"great job"* the designers had done.

Now I've been on a lot planes in my sixty-year career as an entertainer but I can assure you that no plane I had ever been on before, or since, could come close to matching the luxury that had been prepared for Elvis' pleasure inside the cabin of *"The Lisa Marie."*

For this particular engagement, Elvis had brought Lisa Marie in to stay a few days and one night, near the close of her visit, Elvis again came over to our dressing room and told us, *"I'm taking Lisa back to LA after the show and I want y'all to come with me."* As per his norm at a request from Elvis; J. D. answered back, *"Great!."* Soon we were all in transit aboard *"The Lisa Marie"* en route to Hollywood. After a few minutes into the flight I said to Elvis, *"Can I go into the cockpit? I wanna watch 'Elwood Davis' and 'Ron Strause' fly this big bird."* With a big grin Elvis said back to me, *"Sure man! Make yourself at home."*

When we arrived in Hollywood, *"Priscilla"* came on board and greeted all of us and hugged Elvis. After she and Elvis had talked for a while, Elvis walked Priscilla and Lisa Marie to their limo just to make sure that they got safely tucked in.

Ordinarily, Elvis chartered planes for the cast members at the end of a Vegas engagement or a national tour but this particular time in Vegas, he asked us to fly back to Memphis with him on his plane and then he would have his pilots, Elwood Davis and Ron Straus fly us on home to Nashville.

In response to the initial question: *"Yes, I have flown a lot of trips on 'The Lisa Marie'!"*

On numerous occasions, I have also been asked the question, *"How did Elvis get from city to city in such a short period of time."*

The answer is very simple: *"The Lisa Marie!"* It, along with Elvis' smaller jet, that could seat up to ten passengers, were both vital parts of our tour travels across the U.S.

At the start of a tour, Elvis would send his small jet to Nashville to pick up *"The Stamps Quartet."* A chartered flight from Los Angeles would provide transportation for *"Kathy Westmoreland, Glen D. Hardin, Ron Tutt and Jerry Scheff."* The flight would stop over in Las Vegas to board *"Joe Guercio,"* our conductor, along with three of his favorite instrumentalists. Once everyone had arrived at our first tour venue, Elvis turned his small jet over to *"Col. Tom Parker"* who would leave each night and head to the next venue. In tandem with Col. Parker, one additional plane was always seen. It was a big turbo jet that The Colonel had affectionately designated as *"Hound Dog II."* At the successful conclusion of our engagements and after a closing night party during which Elvis would always present each cast member with a nice bonus along with an exquisite gift, the trip back to our homes was exactly like our arriving but in reverse order.

I loved flying *"high and free"* on *"The Lisa Marie"* but it was always good to get back home. However, *"J.D. Sumner,"* the manager, owner and bass singer for *"The Stamps Quartet"* was not known for taking days off. As soon as we arrived back in Nashville, we knew we were about to start a *"gospel tour"* with The Stamps Quartet. There was very little time at home during those days. Most of my time was spend on *"The T.C.B. Bus"* or *"The Lisa Marie."*

I'm still touring as a *"gospel singer"* and I sure wish Elvis was here to fly me to my next engagement:

On *"The Lisa Marie!"*

- Ed Hill

It's O.K To Fly High
as long as

Ya Walk Straight
When Ya Hit The Ground!

Anything For A Laugh

*I*t has often been said that, *"Some folks will do anything for a laugh!"*

"Elvis" and *"Charlie Hodge"* were true *"masters of the art."*

Elvis loved *"J.D. Sumner"* like a brother, and made certain that J.D. was afforded high visibility on every show that they did together.

J.D. was noted for both his captivating stage presence and his style of communicating song lyrics and he was always very serious when endeavoring to relay the lyrical thoughts of a slow gospel tune.

Being aware of this fact, the *"little boy"* in Elvis delighted in trying to cause J.D. to lose his composure during his attempts to be very serious. Suffice it to say; *"With Elvis, serious expressions and mannerisms on stage were a rare commodity."*

With those facts stated, boys and girls; let's stop for a moment and enjoy a case in point.

Elvis was scheduled for two shows a night at the Las Vegas Hilton from August 19, 1974 thru September 2, 1974. During rehearsals for this engagement, Elvis asked *"Joe Guercio,"* his musical conductor and *"Glen D. Hardin,"* his arranger and keyboard man, to arrange *"Kris Kristofferson's"* great song, *"Why Me Lord,"* to feature a solo by *"J.D. Sumner"* on both verses. On numerous occasions I have heard J.D. say, *"I ain't never figured out if Elvis likes my singin' or he just gets a kick out'a tryin' to make me laugh."* Never-the-less, it became Elvis' routine to do or say something during *"Why Me Lord"* that would cause J.D. to lose his demeanor.

The first line of *"Why Me Lord"* reads, *"Why me Lord? What have I ever done to deserve even one of the pleasures I've known?"* Beginning with the songs second performance, it became Elvis' custom to make up a novel answer and in a high pitched lady's voice, speak it out loud enough for J.D. to hear. No one ever knew what Elvis was gonna say and for every show he came up with something different. As you can well imagine, it was always *"extremely funny!"*

During the midnight show on August 21, 1974, Elvis failed to make his usual response to J.D.'s first line in his solo and *"The World's Lowest Bass Singer"* was delighted that he had finally made it thru the first verse to *"Why Me Lord"* without incident and at the closing of J.D.'s solo verse, Elvis proceeded to deliver the song's first chorus in his usual *"heart touching"* style.

As I have stated many times, it was always hard, if not impossible, to determine what was going thru Elvis' mind during his performances and this particular night was no exception. I, for one, began to wonder why Elvis had become so serious at the point where all of the cast had always enjoyed a hearty chuckle.

As Elvis began to sing his first chorus, all the stage lights went dim and the spot light focused on Elvis' head and this was an unusual lighting effect from our lighting director, *"Lamar Fike,"* a cousin to Elvis and a member of the *"Memphis Mafia."* What none of us knew, myself included, was the fact that Elvis had been up to *"mischief"* between the dinner show and the midnight show. It was soon to become very evident why the normal lighting for *"Why Me Lord"* had been changed to a cameo spotlight that was lighting only the head of Elvis.

In the darkness of the moment, *"Charlie Hodge"* was kneeling down at Elvis' feet and was attempting to retrieve something that Elvis had dropped. At least, that's what we all thought. I can assure you that, *"we were very wrong!"*

Everyone in the attendance, including the stage support, became engrossed in Elvis' moving delivery of the song's lyrics. As he sang, Elvis began walking toward the background vocal group to his left. As he moved across the stage, the spotlight got broader and broader. By the time he came to stand in front of the back-up ensemble the spotlight had become wide enough to include Elvis' entire body as-well-as those of all the singers.

Standing directly in front of J.D., Elvis began to sing the last line of the chorus that says, *"Now that I know that I've needed you, so help me Jesus, 'my soul's in your hands'."* As Elvis came to the last phrase of the chorus he lifted his right leg up and stuck it between *"Estelle Brown and Sylvia Shemwell,"* of *"The Sweet Inspirations."* Elvis laid his leg on J.D.'s lap and then we knew what *"Charlie had been doing in the darkness."*

I wish you could have seen what we saw.

Laying there in J.D.'s hands, accentuated by a blazing white spotlight and attached to Elvis stage boot was a *"very large, inflatable, white rubber, clown's foot."*

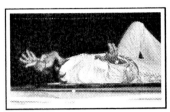

It's no wonder that on that particular performance of *"Why Me Lord," "Joe Guerico"* and the orchestra had a very long instrumental presentation for the second verse and final chorus because there was no way that Elvis nor the singers could get a melodic line out: all of us were *"doubled over with laughter!"*

Later that night, I heard Elvis say to J.D., *"Sorry I messed up your second verse tonight on 'Why Me Lord'."* J.D. answered back, *"No problem, that's probably the best I ever sounded 'cause I wasn't singing."*

Elvis truly loved Gospel music and he insisted on making it a part of every performance and he had an uncanny way of delivering the message of a Gospel song with great respect, while at the same time, using his ability to tease and laugh with J.D. and The Stamps.

I am not sure if Heaven has any laughter but if it does: I am most certain that on numerous occasions; *"Elvis, Charlie Hodge and J.D.,"* are still laughin' about the night *"Elvis stuck his swollen foot into J.D.'s hands."*

"I Know I Am!"

- Ed Hill

Laugh every chance ya get:
It's cheap medicine.

Where's The Beef

*A*nyone lookin' at me can quickly see *"I enjoy eating!"*

Elvis enjoyed eating as well but I can assure you that his dietary demands were different than mine.

During the question and answer moments at my concerts, people often ask, *"What did Elvis like to eat?"*

I generally precede my answer with the comment that *"Elvis was born in Tupelo, Mississippi and raised in Memphis, Tennessee. That fact alone requires a certain taste for 'fried meat and potatoes'."* I am, on the other-hand, from the hills of East Tennessee and *'deep south cooking'* around my parts was a luxury *"only a few were able to enjoy."*

Eating at Elvis' table was much like joining T.V.'s, *"Walton Family,"* at a family reunion in New Orleans, Mississippi. You never knew what to expect but there was always more than enough for everybody and the *"everybodies"* could often be numerous and *"Mary Jenkins Langson,"* Elvis' executive chef for fourteen years, could cook anything they might ask for and in the manner they desired it.

One thing I always found fascinating was Elvis' love for *"fried banana sandwiches"* and *"peanut butter sandwiches."* A jar of peanut butter once enjoyed by Elvis now rests in the *"Elvis and Hollywood Legends Museum"* in *"Pigeon Forge, Tennessee."* It seemed like every time I turned around, Elvis had one or the other, either in his hand or between his teeth. I can also assure you that no one could ever appear as elegant with peanut butter on their chin as could *"my friend, Elvis!"*

At home in Memphis, when the official meal-time rolled around, Mary would always serve Elvis his meals in *"family style bowls"* and might I add, in *"King-size"* portions.

The following is a list that Mary once shared with me of all the items that Elvis required to be in Graceland's food supply at all times: *"Fresh ground round for burgers or meatloaf; Buns, rolls and biscuits; Wieners, sauerkraut, pickles, potatoes, onions, fresh fruit, mustard and* ketchup, Pepsi, orange drinks, whole milk, half & half milk and fresh orange juice."

Elvis loved sweets and wanted the following daily: *"banana pudding, chocolate brownies, fudge cookies, chocolate and vanilla ice cream, shredded coconut,"* and of course, *"peanut butter!"*

Elvis only ate one balanced meal a day. The rest of the time it was *"what-ever"* he wanted from *"where-ever"* he desired it.

Every morning, his main entree was a *"fresh melon"* of some variety and his last food supplement before retiring for the night was always a *"cheeseburger"* from *"The Gridiron Restaurant"* which used to be right down the street from Graceland.

I was always amazed at how much Elvis truly loved The Gridiron's cheeseburgers. It appeared that he would order one at the *"drop of a hat."* On numerous occasions, all the guys would be hangin' out in Graceland's *"jungle room"* and Elvis would holler out, *"Charlie! Call The Gridiron and get us some cheeseburgers!"*

Can you possibly imagine the feeling experienced by some young guy, tending the cash register at the Gridiron, picking up the phone and an unknown voice saying, *"I want four dozen cheeseburgers 'all the way' along with two dozen French fries and deliver 'em to Graceland. When you get to the gate, tell the guard to call 'Charlie Hodge' and I'll have 'im to escort ya to the mansion. I'll be paying with a credit card."*

If I had been the young man I would have been so excited that I would have very quickly washed my hands, cooked a grill full of burgers and in a flash headed for Graceland. He must have been exactly like me because it never took him very long to arrive.

I only recorded at Graceland twice: February 2 thru 9, 1975 and October 29 thru 31, 1976.

During the second of those sessions, we got to Graceland early and Elvis didn't come downstairs for about a couple of hours after we got there.

During our wait, some of the guys would have Mary make them a sandwich of their choice and then go into Graceland's *"pool room"* to play pool or into the *"jungle room"* to watch a movie.

Elvis finally came downstairs and we began the recording session.

About half way thru the session, Elvis called Mary and soon everyone had a *"big bowl of lima beans,"* along with an *"abundant supply of sour milk cornbread."* I thought I had died and gone to heaven. I'm still tryin' to lose the weight that meal created.

"None" of the food in Elvis' kitchen was *"sugar free," "low calorie"* or *"fat free."*

Elvis ate what he wanted to eat, when he wanted to eat it, prepared in the exact manner his southern tastes required.

I'm not certain if Heaven has cheeseburgers but if per-chance they do:

> **I'm certain that Elvis is eating one;**
> **Wrapped in a golden bun.**

- Ed Hill

Description of: Southern Cooking

If It's Healthy
It Ain't Southern

The Final Performance

*"**Y**ou young people need to quit listenin' to all that Rock 'n Roll music. It ain't good for ya!"*

I first heard about *"Elvis Presley"* in the late fifties during a Sunday mornin' message my *"Daddy"* was delivering. He was preachin' on the bad effects of the new *"rock and roll craze"* that was sweepin' the country and how it was damaging the morals of our *"young church folks"*. I remember him, often, using the names *"Elvis Presley"* and *"Jerry Lee Lewis"* in reference to the type of music he was preachin' about.

I have always been an admirer of the female gender and especially so in my teen years but I was *"the preacher's kid"* and consequently I had to be *"Mr. Goodie Two Shoes"* in order to present what my daddy called, *"a good example."* This required no movies, no dancing, no team sports and just basically, *"no fun."* The thought of *"dating"* before I was eighteen was pretty much out of the question. Therefore, my *"girl chasing"* had to be done in my imagination only.

As a side-bar comment: I was once punished for playing *"Checkers"* with my friend next door. Suffice it to say, *"There was no way I was gonna tell Daddy about playing a card game called, 'Old Maid'!"*

Never-the-less, back to my story.

We had a record player at our house but my musical pleasures were limited to Southern Gospel recordings by The Blackwood Brothers Quartet, a world famous Gospel Quartet for whom my Daddy's brother, my Uncle, *"J.D. Sumner, The World's Lowest Bass Singer"* sang bass. The remainder of my record collection was filled with recordings from The Rebels Quartet, another renown Gospel Quartet of the era for whom my Mother's brother, my Uncle, *"John Mathews,"* served as owner and baritone singer.

I can't tell you how many hours I spent sitting in our living room listening to those old Gospel albums but I can certainly tell you that never at any time was there one being played that bore the name, *"Elvis Presley!"*

Between the years 1956 and 1960, my Dad pastored a Pentecostal Church in Easton, Maryland and during 1959, my junior year at the Easton

High School, I had a pretty classmate thatabsolutely loved *"Elvis!"* As the *"nerd"* that I was forced to be, at the time; I had never been able to hear Elvis' music and knew very little about why my friend, Renee, was so fascinated by the man they called, *"Elvis Presley."*

That same year, I had a required class they called Industrial Arts. I always referred to as *"shop class."* At the beginning of the year, I chose as one of my class projects, the building of a *"transistor radio."* It wound up being a simple coil of copper wiring, a battery and a few electronic components resting inside a small wooden box. When my *"boom box"* was completed, I was able to listen to our local radio station via a one piece, handheld earphone. I carried that puppy with me everywhere I went. To me, at that point, it was *"my greatest treasure!"* Not only was it a decent little radio but it also helped me to accomplish one of my teenage goals: *"I started sharing my lunch period with Renee."* All during lunch we would listen to *"rock and roll"* music. We took turns listening as we passed the earphone apparatus back and forth. For the remainder of the school year, Renee and I ate lunch together every day. We would sit at our table with one hand holding a sandwich and the other hand holding an earphone. Renee and my transistor radio quickly made me a fan of *"Elvis Presley!"*

Christmas of 1960 finally arrived and as usual, all *"The Sumners"* gathered at Grandmother's house in Lakeland, Florida to celebrate the season. When it came time to open all the family gifts, I was extremely delighted when I was the recipient of a gift from my *"Uncle Jake"* the world famous, *"J.D. Sumner."*

To my great happiness and to my Father's great surprise, I unwrapped, a just released, record by Uncle Jake's friend, *"Elvis Presley!"* On the cover of the album, Elvis was seated at a piano, much like the one we had in our living room back home. He was dressed in a good looking suit, a white shirt, a tie and might I add, *"a preacher like hair cut!"* As a backdrop for the picture, R.C.A. Records had chosen a church tower with a cross on the front of it. Printed on the album cover was the title, *"His Hand In Mine"* and the credit *"By Elvis Presley!"*

I have yet to determine if it was *"the Cross"* on the cover, Elvis' *"good boy"* picture or the fact that it was *"a gift from Uncle Jake"* but for one of those reasons, Daddy was delighted that I was so happy with my gift. I took the record back home and then later to college. I played it so much that it eventually became so scratchy I had to replace it but one fact remained: it birthed in me an admiration for Elvis that continued to grow and eventually reached a zenith when I was afforded the opportunity to work for him, live with him and call him, *"My Friend!"*

Although he received a large number of musical awards during his career, Elvis only won three *"Grammy Awards"* and all three were for his *"Gospel Recordings:"* *"Best Sacred Performance"* in 1967, *"How Great Thou Art"* in 1972 and *"He Touched Me"* in 1974.

During the years I sang with Elvis, I did a lot of *"Hound Dogs"* and *"Blue Suede Shoes"* but my favorite Elvis songs were the many *"Gospel"* songs he sang. More times than I can remember, I would be singing a Gospel song with Elvis and suddenly have a flashback to 1960 and remember opening up my *"His Hand In Mine"* album by my *"someday to be"* friend, *"Elvis!"*

On August 15, 1977, the night before his death on the 16th, *"Elvis"* and *"Ginger Alden"* went to visit Ginger's mother. As the two of them were preparing to leave for Graceland, Ginger's Mom asked Elvis if he would be so kind as to sing one of her *"favorite Elvis songs"* before he left.

With his normal gracefulness, Elvis walked over to the little spinet piano in their living room, sat down, touched the keyboard and began singing what was to be his *"final performance."*

A tremendous number of questions have been asked and volumes of comments have been offered in regard to the spiritual side of Elvis' living. Some have been kind and others seemed rather cruel but as for me: I lived with him and knew him in the privacy of his own enclosed world. I was made privy to his thoughts and the intents of his heart and this knowledge brings to me great comfort when I view the lyrics that came from his own lips as he sang:

"The last song Elvis would ever sing."

HIS HAND IN MINE

You may ask me how I know
my God is real
You may doubt the things I say
or doubt the way I feel
But I know He's real today, He'll always be
I can feel His hand in mine and
That's enough for me

I will never walk alone, He holds my hand
He will guide each step I take and if I fall
I know He understands
'Til the day He tells me why, He loves me so
I can feel His hand in mine
That's all I need to know

It's also, "Plenty Good Enough For Me!"

- Donnie Sumner

Whosoever Shall Believe Upon Him
Shall Never Perish
but
Shall Inherit Eternal Life.

- John 3:16

The Touch Of His Hand

I wish you could have had the opportunity to see the record player that Elvis used when he was on tour. It was just an *"inexpensive"* little portable player that *"Charlie Hodge,"* Elvis' close friend and right-hand assistant, had purchased for him. It wasn't much to look at but *"it sure brought Elvis a lot of pleasure."*

One of Charlie's responsibilities was *"keeper of the records."* Elvis had a nice collection of Gospel Quartet records that he always wanted close at hand and in-as-much-as Elvis spent a great deal of his time in transit, Charlie created a way by which he could facilitate Elvis' wish. First of all, he went out and found a portable record player that was easy to transport and then he had a *"custom made"* piece of luggage created that would hold and protect Elvis' records when they were on the road.

Elvis' *"Gospel collection"* contained numerous albums by *"The Golden Gate Quartet;"* *"The Blackwood Brothers;"* *"The Statesmen Quartet"* and *"The Sons of Song:"* along with several albums by *"The Foggy River Boys,"* a quartet that *"Charlie Hodge"* had sung in during his young years.

Also included in the collection were a goodly number of *"J.D. Sumner and The Stamps Quartet"* albums but The Stamps albums were in *"a different format"* than the other selections.

In the days when long play, vinyl records were popular, the record companies would furnish the artist with a *"reference pressing"* of their forth coming release. The artist would listen to it in order to insure the correctness of the song sequence as-well-as the overall quality of the

pressing. If all was well, the artist would approve the project and the record manufacturer would proceed with the duplication process.

During my years with The Stamps, it was my uncle J.D.'s practice to send all of the Stamps Quartet's *"reference pressings"* to *"Elvis"* once Uncle Jake had approved them. For that reason, the Stamps albums were the only discs in Elvis' collection without album jackets. All of our records were in place white sleeves with the album title handwritten on the outside.

As a side-bar note: when Elvis *"left the building,"* Charlie Hodge was granted legal possession Elvis' entire Gospel collection. Shortly before Charlie passed away, I was visiting with him in Pigeon Forge, Tennessee and he allowed me to bring the entire set back home with me in order for me to create the entire collection into a digital format. I still have the digital files on my studio computer and often times, when I'm alone in the control room, I'll open one up and have myself a *"listening memory."* Every time I do, I invariably begin to recall the many times *"Elvis, Charlie and I"* would sit together and listen to *"Gospel music."* Thru the eyes of my memory, I can still see Elvis sprawled back in his plush *"listening chair,"* with his feet resting on the footstool and his eyes closed: savoring in the sound of his *"favorite"* form of music.

If you were around Elvis for any length of time, one thing was for sure. You were gonna hear some *"Gospel singing."* It was gonna either

come from a record or from a live voice but you were definitely going to be exposed to the genre.

During my years with *"The Stamps,"* as-well-as my own group *"Voice,"* I had the pleasure of singing an immeasurable number of songs for Elvis, at his request. He used to sit back and just call out song titles for us to sing and we would accommodate his wishes, sometimes, for hours at a time.

Among the list of songs that he most often requested, was a song that my *"Uncle J.D."* and I had both written and recorded with the Stamps Quartet. The song was entitled, *"The Touch Of His Hand"* and it was the title of our album by the same name, released in 1971 on the Heart Warming label. I can't tell you how many times I've sung that song to Elvis, either in his dressing room on tour or in the privacy of his living room at home.

According to my friend, *"Jack Soden, CEO of Elvis Enterprises,"* on the morning of Elvis' death, after the emergency attendants had left his bedroom, they noticed his little portable record player in the corner of his bedroom. The turntable was still spinning and it had reached the end of the record that had been placed on it. The record bore the title, *"J.D. Sumner and The Stamps Quartet 'The Touch Of His Hand'."*

Yes sir! I certainly did sing a lot of songs for *"my friend, Elvis"* but it still brings me a warm feeling way down deep inside when I thoughtfully read the lyrics of what was, in all probability:

"The last song I ever sang to Elvis!"

- Donnie Sumner

THE TOUCH OF HIS HAND

My cup runneth over
My strength is renewed
Though it seems total darkenss for me
Thy rod and Thy staff bring me comfort
At the end there is vict'ry for me

There's a place where I go
To be alone with Jesus
When my burden's too heavy to bear
What strength I find in my trials
What vict'ry in times of despair

Surely goodness and mercy
Is mine each day
On His Word I firmly now stand
Tho I walk thru a valley with a heavy burden
I can feel the touch of His hand

A "Close" Friend

"One is rich, who has friends."

During my seventy plus years of living, I have been made rich by having a multitude of friends. Some are acquaintance friends, others are working companions and then there is small list of *"exceptionally close"* friends. I consider all of these  friendships to be my personal, *"treasure chest of bounty."* Amid the names of all the friends found on the pages of my memories, during the months of *"January and August"* of each year, I am always drawn to *"one"* in particular.

This special friend, to which I have referred, stepped onto the stage of humanity on January 8, 1935. He lived an incredible life and took his final curtain call, early on the morning on August 16, 1977. The world knew him as *"Elvis Presley"* but I remember him as *"Elvis, 'my close friend'."*

To honestly call someone your *"close friend,"* requires the presence of several attributes regarding the relationship.

"Close friend," presupposes the fact that the two persons of interest have spent a great deal of *"quality time together."* For nearly six years, I spent more time with this friend than I did with my family in Nashville, Tennessee. The last year my friend and I were together, I only spent twelve nights in my own home.

 "Close friend," implies a *"mutual respect,"* given each to the other, for the talents and skills they individually possesses. My friend, in point, was a *"super-star"* and I was only a supporting performer. On stage he stood in the spotlight with great poise and expertise while I sat in subdued lighting and endeavored to give my best to the *"boss."* When the lights went dark and the task at hand had been successfully concluded: between the *"two of us,"* there were always, honest and sincere *"compliments of praise"* given along with *"thank you's"* in a host of various forms.

"Close friend," submits the proposition that there is a *"sense of equality"* attributed each to the other. One can be rich and the other of average income; one can be extremely handsome and the other of average countenance; one can be a *"super-star"* and the other just a *"sideman;"*

But between *"close friends"* these characteristics matter not. It's only the knowledge that we both came into this world as *"equals"* and nothing is going to change that fact.

"Close friend," requires *"unconditional acceptance."* It's great being friends when everything is *"sunshine and roses"* but when the *"clouds come"* and the *"wind blows hard"* against the life and living of a friend, the testing of your friendship comes in the manner with which you embrace your friends problem as though it was your own. One numerous occasions, my friend and I have seen each other at a low point. On the other-hand, there were a considerable number of joy-filled moments but regardless of the experience, we both *"listened to each other"* and lived the moments in a *"bond of togetherness."* At no point, was there ever a requirement or a condition that must be met in order to sustain our continued friendship.

"Close friend," contains the built in virtue of *"great loyalty."* A *"close"* relationship cannot built upon *"ifs"* or *"maybes."* A *"true bond of friendship"* remains intact regardless of the situation or circumstance. The loyalty of my friend that I write about, can be summed up in the last words I ever heard him speak. I was leaving to enroll in a drug rehab program in Nashville, Tennessee and as I was saying my good-byes, my friend said to me, *"Man I'm proud of ya. Go do what 'cha have to do and know that I'm here for ya. If there's anything you need or want, just whistle!"*

August has returned for another year and once again I am recalling the years that my *"close friend"* and I enjoyed together. I sit here alone today with just my thoughts and my computer. My fingers are painting pictures of wonderful memories but my eyes miss the portrait of *"my friends smiling face."* My ears miss the sound of *"his laughing"* and my hands feel the absence of *"his handshake."*

I once had a very *"close friend"* and his name was:

ELVIS PRESLEY!

- Donnie Sumner

> The loss of a "Close Friend" saddens the heart
> but
> The promised hope of a "Joy Filled Eternal Reunion"
> brings great
> "Comfort and Peace of Mind!"

Any Man

who has a

TRUE FRIEND

is

RICH

BEYOND MEASURE!

"*I* ain't no saint,
but I've tried
never to do anything that would
hurt my family or offend God.
I figure all any kid needs
is hope and the feeling he or she belongs.
If I could do or say anything
that would give some kid that feeling,
I would believe that
I had contributed something to the world."

Elvis Presley
From a press conference in 1956

Without You
The
Faithful Elvis Fans
The legacy of
Our Friend, "Elvis"
would have become just a faded memory.

"Thank You"
For your friendship
and
For YOUR part
in helping to preserve
the good name of

Elvis Presley:
"The King of Rock and Roll,"
"and the greatest entertainer of all time!"

This Is Not
THE END!

Our Stories Will Continue
when we get together again
with
OUR FRIEND
"ELVIS"

- Donnie Sumner and *Ed Hill*

Ladies and Gentlemen:

"ELVIS
HAS LEFT
THE BUILDING"

"Thank You and Goodnight"